• HALSGROVE DISCOVER SERIES ➤

THE LAKE DISTRICT

Walks from Skiddaw to Scafell

Jerry Rawson

HALSGROVE

LAKE DISTRICT NATIONAL PARK
WALK LOCATIONS

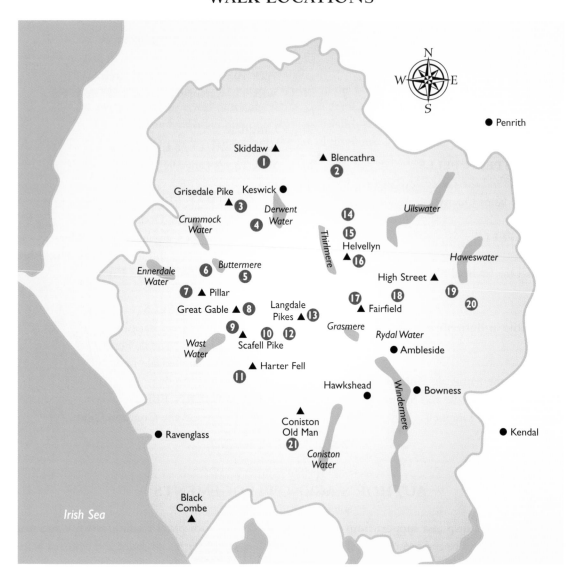

INTRODUCTION

I can still remember my first visit to the Lake District nearly five decades ago as if it was yesterday. Full of youthful enthusiasm, two of us ascended Helvellyn via Striding Edge. It was my first-ever mountain climb, and the one that fired my enthusiasm. I fell in love with the Lake District that day and since then have walked, scrambled, rock-climbed, backpacked, run and skied over the Lakeland fells. The book explores these fells seeking out summits, tarns and lakes, which together make the Lake District such a very special place.

The Lake District, an area of outstanding beauty and perfection of scale, was designated as a National Park in 1951. It lies in Cumbria in the north-west of England and covers 2292 square kilometres/885 square miles. It contains rugged fells, dales, heather moors, lakes, wooded valleys, villages, towns and also parts of the western coastline. Although approximately only 48km/30 miles across, the Lake District contains some of the most spectacular and tightly packed mountain scenery south of the Scottish Highlands.

Ill Crag across Great Moss in Upper Eskdale.

Striding Edge, Helvellyn.

Bowfell, Great Langdale.

The west face of Scafell.

Belles Knott, above Easdale Tarn.

The Helvellyn range from Ullscarf.

Opposite: *The Scafell range from Border End.*

The making of the landscape

The valleys and lakes radiate from a central core of mountains, creating a unique land-scape fashioned by the combined influences of rock-types, submersion, and gigantic upheavals of the earth's crust creating folds and faults. Millions of years of erosion have worn the mountains down to their present size. The major part of the Lake District is made up of three broad bands of rock slanting from south-west to north-east. Skiddaw Slate is the oldest group of rocks, formed during the Ordovician period about 500 million years ago, when mud and layers of silt settled in deep water on the seabed.

About 50 million years later, intense volcanic activity formed the Borrowdale Volcanic Group of lavas and ash south of the Skiddaw Slates. This hard rock makes up the highest and craggiest central mountains, such as the Scafells. To the south, around Coniston and Windermere, an area of slates, silt, sandstones and limestones formed under the sea during the Silurian period about 420 million years ago. These rocks, known as the Windermere Group, are softer, forming a range of gentler hills stretching from the Duddon Estuary to Kendal. The Lake District rocks sit on top of a raft of granite, and small intrusions of this harder rock are seen on the surface in Eskdale and near Keswick.

Haweswater Reservoir and Mardale Head.

The Coniston fells are riddled with old copper mines.

The final shaping of the landscape we see today was mainly brought about by the awesome power of retreating glaciers and their fast-flowing melt-water rivers of the last Ice Age, between 25,000 and 10,000 years ago. The ice ground away rocks, modifying the shape and scale of the mountains, leaving behind U-shaped valleys, combs, glacial lakes, moraines, drumlins and numerous erratic boulders. You can see many of these features along the described walks.

Mining for minerals has also had an impact on the landscape. Graphite was mined near Keswick, leading to the establishment of a pencil industry in the mid sixteenth century. In 1564 Elizabeth I gave royal assent to an Anglo-German venture to mine copper in Borrowdale at the Goldscope Mine. Copper was also mined in Coniston and lead at Glenridding. Many Lakeland rocks have also been quarried, for example, slate at Honister Pass and granite at Threlkeld and Shap. Quarrying still continues, albeit on a smaller scale.

All this industrial activity has left its mark during the last few centuries, and although some of the relics from mining and quarrying still remain, Nature's green mantle is steadily softening the ruins and waste tips, which are still fascinating features along some of the walks.

The impact of people on the landscape

As you walk through the valleys and across the fells it is difficult to imagine that apart from some areas on the high tops and steep crags, nearly all the scenery we have come to enjoy has been influenced at some stage by humans. The landscape is the product of a long history of forest clearance and grazing by sheep. Humans have influenced the landscape stretching back over 10,000 years from when Neolithic people started to clear the forests, settle and farm here, through the Bronze and Iron Ages, the Roman occupation, and the Middle Ages, right up to the present day.

Today, tourism has become the major industry of the Lake District with its associated crowded roads and car parking problems. However, you can usually leave the crowds behind as you head onto the high fells.

The walks

The selected walks explore the main mountain groups (the Northern, North Western, Western, Central, Eastern and Southern Fells) and also reflect their many and varied facets, such as geology, people, history and the working landscape. All the walks are situated within the National Park, and by grouping them into reasonably well-defined geographical areas it means that a trip to any one will usually give a choice of several walks. Walks range from relatively easy ones to some demanding expeditions over wild mountain terrain, where high fitness levels and map and compass skills are essential, especially in bad weather. For weather details see: www.mwis.org.uk; www.lake-district.gov.uk/weatherline or tel: 0870 055 0575.

Walkers on Red Pike above Mosedale.

Although real winter conditions are not as common these days, there are several spells each season when the hills are covered in snow. Then, some of the featureless and inhospitable fells can be very unforgiving for the ill-prepared walker, and the terrain demands respect at all times. However, on clear crisp days with hard snow underfoot, the fells can be exhilarating, not only for walkers but also for ice climbers and ski-tourers.

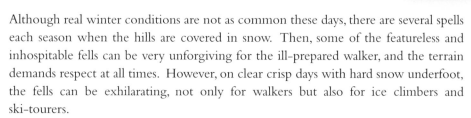

Ski-touring on High Street.

9

Ill Gill, Kirkfell.

A few of the described walks, such as Blencathra's Sharp Edge and Helvellyn's Striding Edge involve some scrambling and are potentially more serious. Scrambling is that adventurous ground where hill-walking and rock-climbing meet. It means that uphill progress involves using your hands as well as feet, often in dramatic situations, where skills and judgment are pre-requisites to a safe passage. Often some of the best ways up Lakeland's mountains involve sections of scrambling.

Scrambles are usually graded on a scale of 1 to 3. Grade 1 routes are relatively straightforward, like Sharp Edge on Blencathra, whereas Grade 2 usually means that you need more technical skills and the terrain is often steeper. Grade 3 scrambles are much more serious, steeper and technical, and involve basic skills in rock climbing plus an ability to use a rope when the terrain demands it; for example Slab and Corner on Pillar Rock.

All scrambling is potentially dangerous, since it is usually done without a rope. As you gain experience you will find that scrambling in Lakeland can provide magnificent days out which last long in the memory. There are several guidebooks for scrambles and if you wish to learn more then it's worth going out with someone experienced or taking a course on basic rope skills at a reputable centre.

The direct finish to Jack's Rake, Pavey Ark.

Pinnacle Ridge, St Sunday Crag.

Grasmere from Loughrigg Fell.

The described walks are on public rights of way, permissive paths or across designated access land and open country. With the implementation of the Countryside and Rights of Way (CROW) Act 2000 in the Lake District, there are now even more areas to explore.

The walks are circular, and covered by the appropriate 1:25000 OS Explorer and Harvey Superwalker maps. The text is merely intended to whet the appetite for a particular area and to encourage the reader to sit down with a map and work out the route details. The times given for the routes are only a general guideline and assume the walk will be undertaken in reasonable weather conditions.

Based on terrain, height ascended and total distance covered, I have indicated the relative seriousness of a walk by grading it Easy, Moderate, Difficult or Very Difficult. I hope this personal choice will encourage readers to go and discover the walks for themselves, and I apologise if your favourite area has been left out.

Most of the starting points for the walks have reasonable parking and many are also accessible by public transport including good rail access along with a network of bus routes. For details use the National Traveline Tel: 0870 608 2608 or www.traveline.org.uk. A wide range of hotels, B&Bs and camping and caravan site accommodation is available; for more details see, www.lake-district.com and www.campingandcaravanclub.co.uk. For information about youth hostel accommodation see www.yha.org. Tourist information is available on www.cumbria-in-the-lake-district.co.uk, at various National Park Information Centres and also the Lake District National Park Authority site at www.lake-district.gov.uk or Tel: 01539 724555.

Pike's Crag, an outlier of Scafell Pike.

Robinson and Crummock Water.

The Langdale Pikes from Lingmoor Fell.

1 NORTHERN FELLS

Sharp Edge, Blencathra.

Cat Bells and Skiddaw.

Rising north of Keswick and Threlkeld are the two giants of the Northern Fells; Skiddaw and Blencathra – also known as Saddleback. The sprawling mass of Skiddaw completely dominates Keswick and the surrounding area. Separating the two hills is a deep fault line through which flows Glenderaterra Beck.

Compared with the rather bland Skiddaw, with its smooth slopes of grass and grey slate screes, Blencathra looks majestic. Blencathra's sculptured southern flanks and soaring ridges put on an enticing display for motorists heading west along the A66 towards Keswick. The finest of these ridges is the knife-edged Sharp Edge, one of the most impressive and demanding ridges in the Lake District.

Both Skiddaw and Blencathra are very popular with walkers, and are usually ascended up their steep southern slopes. In marked contrast, their northern flanks consist of a vast expanse of rolling fells of grass and heather which see few walkers.

The most striking of these fells, which make up the area known as 'Back o'Skidda', are the rolling Ulldale and Calbeck Fells, the most northerly hills in Lakeland. Similarly, north of Blencathra is a vast secluded horseshoe of hills enclosed by Souther and Bowcastle Fells, and backed by Carrock Fell. These quieter fells have the added advantage of often being clear of cloud when the higher tops are cloaked.

The busy town of Keswick is the usual base for exploring the Northern Fells but there are also others including Bassenthwaite, Braithwaite, Threlkeld and several villages in Borrowdale. There are good bus links from Penrith, Ambleside and Windermere. Accommodation is available in numerous B&Bs, hotels, camping barns, youth hostels at Derwent Water and Keswick, along with several campsites in the area. See www.keswick.org

Opposite: *Blencathra reflected in Derwent Water.*

14

WALK 1 SKIDDAW AND ULLOCK PIKE

The view north of Keswick is filled by bulky Skiddaw, which sprawls above the wooded slopes of Latrigg. Of the many ways to the summit the most popular, and easiest, is the tourist route which starts from Keswick and follows a wide stony track over Jenkin Hill and Little Man from where a broad slatey ridge leads up to Skiddaw's summit at High Man. This way was also popular in Victorian times and, according to travel writer Harriet Martineau: 'The ascent of Skiddaw is easy, even for ladies, who have only to sit on their ponies to find themselves at the top after a ride of six miles.' There was even a refreshment hut halfway up the track.

The most popular route though is not always the most attractive or challenging. For that you need to head west. This described walk, starting from the hamlet of Bassenthwaite, involves a long ascent of a well-defined ridge over Ullock Pike and Longside Edge to Carl Side before climbing up scree slopes to the top of Skiddaw.

The return leg is north via Bakestall and the valley of Dash Beck. It's an excellent walk with superb views throughout. The initial and final stages near Bassenthwaite, pass through a pastoral landscape of fields surrounded by hedgerows, and are in marked contrast with the rocky slopes and bare summit ridges of Skiddaw.

Bassenthwaite lies just east of the top end of Bassenthwaite Lake which, apart from being the only 'lake' in the Lake District (all the others are known as 'meres' or 'waters'), is also now well known for its ospreys which have nested in woods here for a number of years, usually rearing several chicks each season. The lake, and part of the adjacent shoreline, is a National Nature Reserve with other large areas being Sites of Special Scientific Interest. Unusually, the reserve is wholly owned and run by the Lake District National Park Authority.

Skiddaw from Long Side.

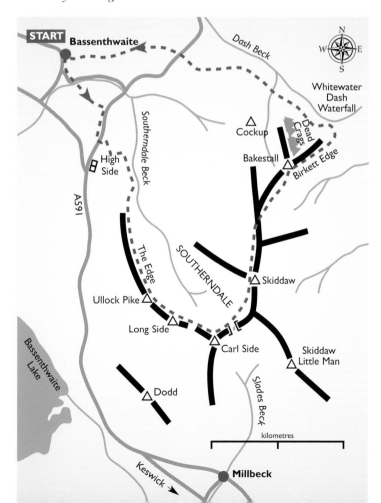

Skiddaw overlooking Keswick.

Bassenthwaite to High Man

The day starts from a minor road just south of the village green where a series of paths cross fields south-east towards Skiddaw, which dominates the skyline ahead. Once across a footbridge over Chapel Beck, a path climbs through pastures to eventually reach a minor road from Orthwaite. About 300m/330 yards right is a lay-by (an alternative starting point for the walk) just above High Side. From here a signed Public Bridleway slants up left across grassy slopes, past a row of ancient hawthorns, before curving right to a track running into Southerndale valley.

Skiddaw from Keswick.

The Edge, Ullock Pike.

Leaving Carl Side for Skiddaw.

Branching right from the track you arrive at the foot of a well-defined ridge, known as The Edge. A path leads up over numerous rises, passing an awkward craggy section just before reaching the high point of Ullock Pike. Beyond here the narrow ridge sweeps up Longside Edge towards the rocky top of Long Side and provides superb walking along its crest from where you have fine views right of Bassenthwaite Lake backed by Sale Fell and Lord's Seat, while to the left, broken crags and steep scree slopes plunge down to Southerndale.

After a short descent the wide path traverses across the grassy left flank of Carl Side, whose summit is easily reached by a short detour. The top of Carl Side (746m/2447 feet) is a great viewpoint and is overlooked by Skiddaw's scree slopes to the north and separated from Skiddaw Little Man to the east by Slade Beck's deep, wide gorge.

To the west across green flatlands is the distant Cumbrian coastline and the Irish Sea, while further right is the Solway Firth and Scotland. The bird's-eye-view south across the patchwork of fields around the River Derwent and Keswick, with Derwent Water backed by a wide skyline of peaks is superb.

From Carl Side the main path is rejoined by descending north-east to a col and the small, often dry, Carlside Tarn from where you have a great retrospective view of Longside Edge. Straight ahead is the obvious steep eroded path up the huge mound of splintered slate on Skiddaw's western flank.

The ascent is hard work but you eventually emerge onto the long and stony summit ridge of Skiddaw, which is followed north to the cairn, viewpoint table and trig column at 931m/3054 feet. Here the views really open up, especially to the rolling hills, ridges and valleys to the east and south. After the steep slog up scree slopes, first time visitors are often surprised by the much gentler, rolling moorlands and hills to the north, known as 'Back o'Skidda'. Here are to be found tops with intriguing names such as Willy Knott, Cockup, Little Cockup and Great Cockup.

Skiddaw reflected in Bassenthwaite Lake.

Crossing Long Side backed by Bassenthwaite Lake.

Skiddaw to Bassenthwaite

Stony slopes now lead down to the North Top and on towards the plateau of Broad End, where a wire fence is followed right along to the summit cairn of Bakestall. Straight ahead and below are Dead Crags overlooking the valley of Dash Beck. After traversing the rim of the crag, a descent along Birkett Edge lands you at a stony pack-horse track coming over from Skiddaw House.

Across the track is the head of Dash Beck and Dash Falls (named Whitewater Dash on OS maps). The falls tumble over a steep cliff into a narrow ravine and are one of the best sets of cascades in the Lake District, especially after heavy rain. With care, steep paths can be descended alongside the falls from where you can peer into the various cascades.

Approaching the summit of Skiddaw.

The track drops steeply north-west into the valley, passing below the impressive Dead Crags on whose right-hand side is Dead Beck with its own set of fine cascades. Eventually the tarmaced track for Dash Farm is reached, which leads in about 1km/0.6 mile to the Orthwaite Road.

If you started from High Side, then you turn left here and follow the road, then a bridleway past the farm at Barkbeth to the lay-by. Otherwise you cross the road and continue along the bridleway signed for Bassenthwaite. After a short distance along the track to Peter House Farm, the waymarked bridleway branches off left passing through a series of field paths back to Bassenthwaite's village green and welcome refreshments.

INFORMATION

Start/Finish: Bassenthwaite car park opposite the Sun Inn GR: 230323.
Distance: 15km/9.3 miles.
Walking Time/total climb: 900m (2953 feet)/7 hours.
Grading: Difficult; a high level fell walk on mainly good paths. Under snow and ice the steep slopes leading up to Skiddaw require care.
Maps: OS Explorer OL4, North-western area; Harvey Superwalker, Lakeland North.
Refreshments: Sun Inn, Bassenthwaite.
Public Transport: Railway station at Penrith with regular bus link to Keswick, from where a bus service along the A591 passes near Bassenthwaite.

Negotiating the tricky heights of Sharp Edge.

WALK 2 BLENCATHRA AND SHARP EDGE

Though relatively short, a traverse of Blencathra via Sharp Edge returning down Halls Fell is a magnificent mountain day, and can easily be varied to suit weather and inclination. If a scramble along Sharp Edge seems too daunting then there are several alternatives. The walk also provides excellent views into the heart of the Lake District.

Blencathra stands in splendid isolation about 8km/5miles east of Keswick, and few other Lakeland peaks present such an appealing sight from a distance. When seen from the east, Blencathra has a distinctive saddle shape which gives it its alternative name of 'Saddleback.' Its impressive and symmetrical south face consists of three matching rocky ridges bounded by a pair of grassy buttresses alternating with four scree-choked, deep V-cut ravines with bilberry and heather flanks. Low down the ridges are blunt but their upper crests are rocky, steep and narrow, sweeping up to pointed tops.

All three ridges provide interesting approaches to Blencathra's scalloped summit crest. However, it is Hall's Fell, the central ridge whose upper section is known as Narrow Edge and ends abruptly at the actual summit, which is the most exciting, though a vertical ascent of 700m/2300 feet in 1.6km/1 mile is a bit challenging.

On the eastern flank of Blencathra is a secluded ice-scalloped rocky combe, which cradles the dark waters of Scales Tarn overlooked to the north by the knife-edge rocky arête of Sharp Edge, arguably Lakeland's finest and narrowest ridge.

Threlkeld to Blencathra

Starting from the lovely village of Threlkeld, once a Celtic hamlet and later a mining village, you head north-east towards the A66 Penrith – Keswick road to join a lane leading left to Gategill farm and the open

20

Blencathra across Derwent Water.

fellside. Above the farm, a worn path leads right to start the traverse across the lower slopes of Blencathra.

The path contours across the hillside crossing the series of gills descending from stony ravines. Above the hamlet of Scales, the path steadily climbs diagonally across the hillside eventually rising steeply over the shoulder of Scales Fell to a wide saddle above the hollow of Mousethwaite Comb. Ahead rears the distant imposing profile of Foule Crag on Atkinson Pike, with the crest of Sharp Edge below it looking quite daunting.

Blencathra's summit ridge.

An almost level path now contours along the left flank of the narrow Glenderamackin valley high above the river. At Scales Beck a steep stony path climbs up left into an impressive combe containing Scales Tarn, overlooked by a steep headwall and bounding ridges. On the right-hand side of the combe are the shattered rocks of Foule Crag and the narrow fin of Sharp Edge, now appearing less intimidating. Surrounded by steep craggy slopes, Scales Tarn is in shadow most of the time and is said to be the coldest tarn in Lakeland.

Approaching Sharp Edge from Scales Tarn.

The start of Sharp Edge.

Left: *Superb scrambling on Sharp Edge.*

This is a good place for a rest while deciding on the choice of route from here. If Sharp Edge doesn't appeal, or the weather is poor, then you have several options. One of them is to follow a path up the steep north-eastern slopes above Scales Tarn, joining Scales Fell ridge just below the summit plateau. Alternatively, at the foot of Scales Beck continue along the path to the head of Glenderamackin valley before striking left up grass and the Blue Screes to the top of Foule Crag and nearby Atkinson Pike.

For Sharp Edge an obvious worn path swings right from the tarn up a grassy spur to rockier terrain and the start of the narrow ridge. The horizontal crest of Sharp Edge is Lakeland's equivalent to Snowdonia's Crib Goch arête and, like its counterpart, is classed as a Grade 1 scramble and is also very exposed. For many walkers this is a great introduction to scrambling although you need a good head for heights. The ridge sweeps away steeply on both sides in a series of drops over crags and scree and in strong winds, a crossing of Sharp Edge can quickly become an epic. In dry conditions on a calm day the traverse is straightforward enough, but when wet, the slate becomes slippery and care is needed. Cloaked in snow and ice the ridge becomes a proper winter climb where a rope, axe and crampons may be required.

Scramblers can stick to the very crest of the ridge along slabs, pinnacles and roof-like ridges while walkers have the easier option of a path on the right side. There is no

Sharp Edge and Foule Crag dominate the upper Glenderamackin valley.

The sculptured flanks of Blencathra.

A winter ascent of Halls Fell.

South to the Dodds from the top of Halls Fell.

INFORMATION

Start/Finish: Car park at Threlkeld GR: 323254.

Distance: 10km/6 miles.

Walking Time/total climb: 5 hours/750m (2461 feet).

Grading: Very Difficult; a strenuous fell walk on mainly good paths but with some steep ascents and descents, and some Grade 1 scrambling.

Maps: OS Explorer OL5, North-eastern area; Harvey Superwalker, Lakeland North.

Refreshments: Inns at Threlkeld, White Horse Inn at Scale and cafés and pubs in Keswick.

Public Transport: Regular bus service between Penrith and Keswick along the A66.

real escape from the rocks because all routes meet at a notch, the crossing of which is the most difficult part of the ridge and involves a couple of tricky steps across slabby rocks, precarious when wet, on the right-hand side of a leaning pinnacle which effectively blocks the way.

Beyond the notch, the sharp horizontal ridge abuts against the tilted slabby rocks of Foule Crag. The headwall rears up and the easiest line of weakness is up a trench-like series of grooves just to the right, though the rocks straight above are excellent and easier than first appearances suggest. Both ways are well-scratched and steep at first but then ease after about 30m/98 feet at a ledge from where a path leads up left to the top of Atkinson Pike. The way is now south-west across close-cropped grass into a dip, passing a large memorial cross made of white quartz rocks piled on the ground, and around the rim of the combe above Tarn Crags up to Hallsfell Top, the high point on Blencathra, its top crowned by an insignificant cairn at 868m/2848 feet and a low circular trig point.

The view north-west across to the Solway Firth and the Scottish hills beyond is very appealing. But the southerly aspect across the deep green vale to the panorama of Lakeland fells ranging from High Street and Helvellyn, to Scafell and the hills beyond Derwent Water is unsurpassed.

Blencathra to Threlkeld

Narrow Edge at the top of Halls Fell now drops south from Blencathra's summit. It's decision time; a steep descent of Hall's Fell, or a traverse of the wave-like crest of the summit ridge over Gategill Fell Top, Blencathra's western summit, and on to the top of Blease Fell, before an easier descent down the grassy slopes below Knowe Crags to meet a path leading back to Threlkeld.

The initial descent of Narrow Edge down a grassy buttress is very steep and then, as the angle eases, the crest becomes narrow and rocky. The path weaves its way over and around outcrops avoiding most difficulties, although a couple of short, rocky steps need care. The path eventually swings right and descends through bracken and heather to the wall at the foot of Gategill ravine. Here the outward route is joined back to Threlkeld.

Sharp Edge in profile.

Below left: *Sharp Edge from Foule Crag.*

Below right: *Scales Fell's twisting ridge.*

Approaching Maiden Moor backed by Derwent Water.

2 NORTH WESTERN FELLS

West of Derwent Water is a range of rolling grass and heather-covered fells bordered by Buttermere and Crummock Water, Borrowdale and the Whinlatter Pass, which connects the village of Braithwaite with the Vale of Lorton. This is Derwent's triangle of Skiddaw slate, whose eastern flanks are penetrated by the deep troughs of the Coledale and Newlands valleys.

It is a landscape which offers challenging circular walks along exposed ridges linking shapely peaks from which you get wonderful vistas across the surrounding fells and into valleys. The dominant peak is Grasmoor, whose western slopes sweep up above Crummock Water. But it is the pyramidal-shaped Grisedale Pike, overlooking Whinlatter Pass to the north, which is the most appealing. One of the classic views hereabouts is across Derwent Water to Cat Bells.

Beyond Whinlatter Pass and bordered by Lorton Vale, Bassenthwaite Lake and the Vale of Cockermouth is a vast area of dense conifer forest backed by a series of gentle heather moorland fells. The most prominent of these are the smooth, rounded hills of Lord's Seat, Broom Fell, Sale Fell and Ling Fell. Once you penetrate the heart of this area, usually via Aiken valley which rises above Spout Force and Whinlatter Pass, or the lovely green valley of Wythop in the north, you can find real solitude.

Some of the north-western fells were once an important part of Lakeland's mining history going way back before the Tudors, when metals such as lead, copper, and silver formed an important part of the local economy. This legacy of decay with its scattered industrial remains adds extra interest to the walks.

Centres for exploring the North Western fells include Keswick, Braithwaite, Newlands, Lorton Vale and Borrowdale from where there are good bus links with Penrith, Ambleside and Windermere. Accommodation is available in numerous B&Bs, hotels, camping barns, youth hostels at Derwent Water and Keswick, along with several campsites in the area. See www.keswick.org

Robinson reflected in Crummock Water.

Causey Pike and the Derwent Fells from Cat Bells.

Grisedale Pike seen across Coledale Hause.

WALK 3 GRASMOOR AND THE COLEDALE RIDGES

One of the best skyline walks in the area is around the rim of the Coledale valley just south-west of Braithwaite. It is a challenging circular walk along exposed ridges linking the impressive tops of Grisedale Pike, Hopegill Head, Grasmoor and Crag Hill from where you have wonderful views across the north-west fells and into the heart of central Lakeland.

Braithwaite to Grasmoor

Starting from a small car park about 200m/218 yards up the B5292 Whinlatter Pass road from Braithwaite, a well-signed path for Grisedale Pike is followed up its long north-east ridge overlooking the vast forest plantations to the right. As height is steadily gained up the steep heathery ridge, Derwent Water comes into view to the left, along with the wide valley stretching east beyond Keswick.

With the pyramid-shaped Grisedale Pike having such a lofty and isolated top situated at 791m/2595 feet, it's not surprising that on a clear day you are rewarded with fine views, especially south across Coledale to Causey Pike, Sail and Eel Crag and north-east to the bulky Skiddaw. Immediately below, to the north, are the Whinlatter and Thornthwaite Forests, backed by the moorland domes of Lord's Seat and Broom Fell.

Leaving Grisedale Pike, a path leads round to Hopegill Head (770m/2525 feet) also known as Hobcarton Pike, whose narrow summit is the culminating point of several ridges. One of these ridges leads north to Ladyside Pike

Above left: *Looking up Sail Beck to Sail and Causey Pike.*

Above right: *The view from Hopegill Head to Whiteside.*

across some easy angled but airy slabs, poised high above the cirque of Hobcarton Crag. These dark, crumbling and vegetated shaley cliffs are a favourite with adventurous botanists seeking out the elusive red alpine catchfly, *Viscaria alpina*, one of Britain's rarest flowers. If time permits, a short out-and-back detour to Ladyside Pike is worthwhile for the fine view across to Grisedale Pike.

South of Hopegill Head a shaley path leads over Sand Hill and down to the broad, grassy saddle of Coledale Hause between Crag Hill and Hopegill Head. Throughout the descent your eyes will be drawn to the crumbling face of Eel Crag straight ahead on the lower slopes of Crag Hill, with the bulky Grasmoor to the right – the undoubted monarch of the range.

Heading from Grisedale Pike to Hopegill Head.

An ascent of Grasmoor initially involves heading south up the path from the col, then crossing the beck and climbing a steep path up the eastern slopes to the top of Dove Crags. From here it's just a gentle stroll across to the summit at 852m/2795 feet. The steep climb up Grasmoor is worth the effort just for the fine panorama from its summit, especially to the south across Crummock Water to Red Pike and High Crag backed by the impressive front of Scafell, Gable and Pillar – Lakeland's majestic triptych.

South from Grasmoor into the heart of Lakeland.

Tower Ridge, a scrambler's approach to Crag Hill.

Grasmoor to Braithwaite

Returning back east across the plateau, a well-defined footpath leads down to a swampy depression, on the other side of which a grassy path slants south-east up to the top of Wandope. Standing at 772m/2533 feet, you have breathtaking panoramic views from the summit. Just under the north-eastern flank of Wandope is the superb deep hanging valley of Addacombe Hole, one of the finest in the Lake District.

A path now leads north round the rocky rim before heading up to the summit of Crag Hill at 839m/2751 feet, more commonly known as Eel Crag. In fact Eel Crag is really the name of the rugged northern ridge-end above Cauldale Hause. Crag Hill can also be approached up the deeply-cut Coledale, via an easy scramble up the well-defined Tower Ridge. The ridge forms part of a triangular feature of rock on the north face of Eel Crag up the hillside beyond the ruined buildings and spoil heaps of the old Force Crag Mine. This was the last working mine in the National Park, where barytes was extracted until as recently as 1991.

From Crag Hill you now head east and descend a worn, stony path down a steep ridge leading to a narrow col, beyond which the path climbs gently up to the rounded heather and grassy dome of Sail at 773m/2536 feet. With the Skiddaw range visible ahead, the steep path drops to the col between Sail and Scar Crags.

The main path continues east towards Causey Pike but our way is north-east towards Coledale down a steep rocky path, which traverses a narrow ledge across Scar Crags precipitous north-western flank. Just below Scar Crags on the Coledale side is an abandoned cobalt mine, and opposite, on the other side of the valley, you can pick out the old Force Crag Mine, backed by Grisedale Pike.

When the path eventually levels out on High Moss a faint trod leads over marshy ground across the flanks of Outerside with Causey Pike to the right. The path descends between the two peaks then skirts round the eastern-side of Stile End to the gap of Barrow Door. Here, a well-trodden path takes you down left through heather overlooking Barrow Gill's tumbling stream, and ends with a long and gentle grassy descent through bracken-covered slopes.

A steep descent from Eel Crag towards Sail.

Above: *Grisedale Pike from Hopegill Head.*

Left: *Crossing the northern flank of Scar Crags.*

After passing through a gate a steep road leads left, eventually passing Coledale Inn's front door and the option of slaking your thirst. Beyond the inn the road curves sharply right where you branch off left alongside a row of cottages. Turning left after the cottages you then head right to cross a footbridge over Coledale Beck from where a path leads to the B5292 road near the car park and the end of the walk.

INFORMATION

Start/Finish: Small car park off the B5292 Whinlatter Pass road, 200m/220 yards west of Braithwaite village, GR: 227237.

Distance: 14.5km/9 miles.

Walking Time/total climb: 6 hours/1000m (3280 feet).

Grading: Difficult; a high mountain walk along mainly well-marked paths across a mixture of craggy terrain, narrow ridges and easy slopes but with some steep ascents.

Maps: OS Explorer OL 4; Harvey Superwalker, Lakeland West.

Refreshments: Three pubs in Braithwaite; various cafés and pubs in nearby Keswick.

Public Transport: Braithwaite served by bus from Keswick to Cockermouth.

The summit of High Spy.

Opposite page: *Robinson and High Snab Bank rising beyond Little Town.*

WALK 4 THE NEWLANDS QUARTET

The hamlet of Little Town is famous for two things: Beatrix Potter, and the starting point for a walk around the Newlands valley. This excellent walk tackles the rugged skyline along exposed ridges linking the quartet of Robinson, Hindscarth, Dale Head and High Spy. Apart from some wonderful views, the walk is also rich in historical associations.

From Braithwaite, narrow hill roads lead west to Little Town, passing the farm at Uzzicar in the heart of the Newlands valley. Here once lay a stretch of water known as Uzzicar Lake which was drained by the monks of Furness in the thirteenth century to expose cultivable land; hence the name 'New Lands'.

The famous children's author Beatrix Potter was a frequent visitor to Little Town, which appears in *The Tale of Mrs Tiggy-Winkle*. The character of Lucie of Little Town is supposed to have been based on the daughter of the vicar at Newlands church. Beatrix Potter used the income from her books to invest in hill farms and left 4000 acres of land to the National Trust when she died in 1943.

It is difficult to appreciate that this quiet corner of the Newlands valley was once an important centre for mining. Situated just up the valley near Low Snab Farm was one of the most important mines in Lakeland – the Goldscope Mine.

In 1563 mining experts from Germany took control of the mine (Goldscope is thought to be a corruption of a German word *Gottesgab*, meaning 'God's gift'). Copper and lead were mined as well as smaller quantities of silver and there was a large smelting works on the shore of Derwent Water. It was the richest copper mine known at the time and was considered important enough

Newlands church backed by the Derwent fells.

for Queen Elizabeth I to requisition it for the Crown when it became part of The Company of Mines Royal in 1565. In 1852 a rich lead vein was discovered, which for the next decade made it a very prosperous mine.

Little Town to Dale Head

From Chapel Bridge spanning Newlands Beck, a leafy lane leads south-west past Newlands church, eventually climbing alongside Keskdale Beck past the drive to High Snab Farm to Low High Snab. About 200m/220 yards beyond here, past a cottage, a path branches right, climbing steeply through grass and bracken to gain the top of High Snab Bank. Turning left here the ridge is ascended steeply to Blea Crags where there is a stretch of easy scrambling up a few rocky steps and knolls.

Continuing up the straightforward narrow ridge you arrive at the domed summit of Robinson at 737m/2418 feet, which offers some grand views of the Derwent fells and west across the Buttermere valley to the High Stile-High Crag range.

Leaving Robinson's summit descend south to the narrow ridge of Littledale Edge linking Robinson and Hindscarth. The undulating grassy ridge swings south-east to eventually meet another ridge branching north to Hindscarth. As you head across the broad connecting ridge to Hindscarth (727m/2385 feet) the hill appears quite insignificant, but not so from the Newlands valley where a long, steep spur rises above Scope End and the abandoned tunnels and spoil heaps of the disused Goldscope Mine. The spur provides a connoisseur's approach to the tops. It's worth a short walk north from the summit to a large stone shelter from where you can really appreciate the view down into the Newlands valley.

After retracing your steps back to the main ridge, the way is now south-east along Hindscarth Edge towards Dale Head. Along this stretch the Buttermere valley opens up behind and you have a bird's-eye-view down to the Honister Pass road. Although gentle at first, the ridge eventually steepens, becoming rocky and narrow in places before reaching the summit cairn at 753m/2470 feet.

The High Stile fells from Hindscarth.

Crossing Hindscarth Edge.

South-west from Dale Head to Fleetwith Pike and Pillar.

Forming a junction between the hard Borrowdale volcanic rocks and the soft Skiddaw slates, Dale Head is a fascinating place. From beside the tall summit cairn which clings to the very edge of the steep northern flanks, the ground sweeps away below your feet to the open, green valley bottom, flanked by the dark, rugged crags of High Spy and Maiden Moor ridge to the east and Hindscarth's craggy slopes to the west. The glaciated U-shaped valley and ridges lead your eyes to the wide green Vale of Keswick backed by the bulk of Skiddaw.

The dip between High Spy and Dale Head.

The Newlands valley and Skiddaw from Dale Head.

Dale Head to Little Town

The next objective is High Spy, which is approached down a steep, pitched stony path which soon turns sharp right above a cliff, before weaving its way down steep grassy slopes to Dalehead Tarn situated in a grassy hollow where the valley path from Buttermere joins the one from Newlands (a good escape route). Once across the beck on the left of the tarn an obvious path climbs steeply up grassy slopes to High Spy. The long, narrow rocky ridge of High Spy, its high point at 653m/2143 feet, is a fine vantage point, sitting high above the mile-long crumbling precipices of Eel Crag, overlooking the Newlands valley, while its eastern slopes drop into the Jaws of Borrowdale.

Crossing High Spy.

Leaving the top of High Spy, the path continues north along the broad ridge, gradually descending in a series of steps to cross Maiden Moor, then continuing down steep grass to Hause Gate, the depression before the popular summit of Cat Bells. All along this section you can look back with satisfaction across the Newlands valley to the fells visited earlier in the day; but it is the view across Derwent Water to Skiddaw and Blencathra which will probably claim your attention.

At Hause Gate you simply turn left and follow a bridleway, initially down steep scree slopes, back to the hamlet of Little Town. If you want to extend the day a bit further then why not continue north over Cat Bells, one of the most popular and easiest high level viewpoints in the Lake District. After descending the north ridge of Cat Bells to Hawes End, a track can be followed left past Skelgill back to Little Town.

The Derwent Fells from Maiden Moor.

INFORMATION

Start/Finish: Car park at Chapel Bridge about 400m/435 yards south-west of Little Town, GR: 232194.

Distance: 15km/9.3 miles.

Walking Time/total climb: 6 hours/ 835m (2740 feet).

Grading: Moderate; mainly easy walking on clear paths; a steep descent from Dale Head.

Maps: OS Explorer OL 4; Harvey Superwalker, Lakeland West.

Refreshments: Various pubs in Braithwaite.

Public Transport: Nearby Braithwaite served by bus from Keswick and Cockermouth.

Walkers on Maiden Moor.

Heading for Cat Bells from Maiden Moor.

The ferry on Derwent Water.

Approaching the summit of Combe Head.

3 WESTERN FELLS

This huge area of fells contains many of the most rugged and best-known mountains in Lakeland; the Scafells, Great Gable, the Langdale Pikes, Bowfell, Pillar, Grasmoor and many others. There are also a series of stunning valleys, which penetrate into the heart of the area, including Borrowdale, the Buttermere valley, Eskdale, Wasdale and Ennerdale, some of them containing beautiful lakes such as Wast Water and Buttermere.

BORROWDALE

The steep-sided glacial valley of Borrowdale runs south from Keswick towards some of the highest and craggiest fells in Lakeland. The valley, with its forested crags, oak woods and wonderful lake and river scenery, is arguably one of the most beautiful in the Lake District. On the minus side, the Borrowdale area also has the highest rainfall in England.

Derwent Water fills the lower and wider reaches of the valley, before the dale narrows at the Jaws of Borrowdale, near the hamlet of Grange. Beyond the constriction, the dale opens up again to reveal rich walled pastures spread across the flat valley floor overlooked by a huge group of fells at the valley head. Here the valley divides to become Langstrath to the east and Seathwaite to the west. There are some lovely hamlets here including Rosthwaite, Stonethwaite, Seatoller and Seathwaite. The head of the valley forms a natural horseshoe around Styhead Pass, providing a gateway to the higher tops such as the Scafells, Great Gable and Bowfell. There are also numerous low-level walks around Derwent Water, which can be linked by ferry.

A regular bus service runs between Keswick and Seatoller and walkers are urged to use this to help reduce the major car parking problems in the area. There is plenty of accommodation in the valley including B&Bs, hotels, youth hostels at Longthwaite, Derwent Water and Honister Pass, and campsites at Seathwaite and Stonethwaite. See also www.borrowdale.com.

Left: *A view into Borrowdale from Thornythwaite Fell.*

Great Gable seen from Glaramara.

Left: *Walkers in Gillercombe above Seathwaite.*

WALK 5 AROUND THE STYHEAD SKYLINE

The charming hamlet of Seatoller at the foot of Honister Pass is the starting point for this skyline walk, around two undulating ridges linked by the low pass at Styhead, situated between Great Gable and Great End. It's a challenging walk taking in the long ridge across Glaramara and Allen Crags to Esk Hause and then descending to Styhead Pass. This involves losing a lot of hard-gained height before the long pull up Great Gable, finally returning along the broad ridge across Green Gable, Brandreth and Grey Knotts to Honister Hause followed by a gentle stroll back down to Seatoller.

The summit of Combe Head.

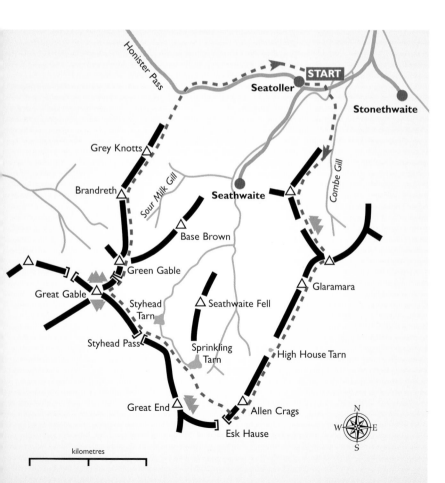

Seatoller to Glaramara

Our day starts at the National Trust car park at Seatoller, from where the B5289 road is followed back towards Keswick to a bridge over the River Derwent. Just beyond the bridge a farm lane heads off right and after about 100m/110 yards a path slants up left through bracken and scattered woodland, to arrive at a grassy area just above Combe Gill with its fine waterfalls. This is a magnificent spot overlooked by the craggy slopes and rocky skyline of Rosthwaite Fell to the left, the great amphitheatre of The Combe straight ahead, and Thornythwaite Fell soaring up to the right.

A stony path climbs steeply up towards Thornythwaite Fell and as height is gradually gained you can peer left into The Combe with the impressive Raven Crag visible just below the summit of Combe Head. The path continues over Capel Crag and follows the crest of Thornythwaite Fell towards the rocky northern slopes of Glaramara, not yet visible at this stage.

The Great Gable – Brandreth Ridge from Combe Head.

Before crossing a broad grassy col to Glaramara, it's worth making a short detour left up a faint path and rocky slopes to Combe Head, its summit at 735m/2411 feet crowned with a cairn. From this lofty position on the very edge of steep craggy slopes sweeping down into The Combe, you can look north to Derwent Water backed by Skiddaw and Blencathra, while just to the right is the complex roller-coaster ridge linking Combe Head with Rosthwaite Fell and the small pointed peak of Bessyboot.

To the south-west, across the broad hollow dotted with numerous small lakes, lies the craggy eastern face of Glaramara. Descending south-east from Combe Head, a faint path meanders round the left-hand side of the tarns towards Glaramara. You can either contour round the crags to the left and follow a rocky ridge to the summit, or head right to rejoin the main path and climb an obvious rocky gully splitting the craggy face. Either way you arrive at Glaramara, its rocky summit at 783m/2569 feet topped by a cairn and windbreak. Once again the views are superb, especially of Great and Green Gables.

The craggy north face of Glaramara.

Approaching the top of Glaramara.

Glaramara to Great Gable

Just south are Glaramara's two subsidiary tops, which are easily visited on the way to Allen Crags. This section of the circuit follows the crest of an undulating ridge over the minor tops of Looking Stead, Red Beck Top and High House Tarn Top. You also pass a number of tarns along this enjoyable stretch, the most memorable being High House Tarn which acts as a lovely foreground for a view across to the Langdale Pikes. A steep climb finally lands you at the top of Allen Crags (785m/2575 feet), with the craggy north-east face of Great End split by deep gullies filling the skyline ahead and blocking out views of the Scafell range.

West from Glaramara to Great and Green Gables.

Great End seen from Glaramara.

Great and Green Gables from near Sprinkling Tarn.

Wasdale from the summit of Great Gable.

Ennerdale from Green Gable.

Descending Green Gable towards Brandreth.

South-east from Grey Knotts to Great End.

From Allen Crags the path drops south-west to meet the main path from Esk Hause and then continues below the slopes of Great End towards the broad shelf of Seathwaite Fell and Sprinkling Tarn, a lovely spot for refreshments. After skirting around the northern spur of Great End, you finally arrive at Styhead Pass, crossed by the ancient track linking Wasdale with Borrowdale. Ahead, the dome of Great Gable beckons and the way is straight up the obvious constructed path rising steeply beyond a mountain rescue box.

Great Gable (899m/2949 feet) is one of the most uniformly steep peaks in the Lake District with crags and screes almost encircling the mountain, creating a feeling of isolation. It's a long steady plod up the path but the effort is worthwhile for the magnificent panoramic views from its summit. Countless walkers have stood here and looked out beyond the huge Westmorland Cairn, a mere stone's throw south-west of the summit, and enjoyed the classic view down the full length of Wasdale backed by the Irish Sea. Set in the rocks near the cairn is a war memorial to members of the Fell and Rock Climbing Club.

Great Gable to Seatoller

Leaving Great Gable's summit, a stony path leads north-east across the plateau before plunging down rocky slopes and scree to the narrow saddle of Windy Gap, followed by a short climb up a rocky path to the top of Green Gable at 801m/2628 feet. Not surprisingly the views are superb, especially back to the precipitous north face of Gable and further right into Ennerdale with Pillar and the sharp profile of Pillar Rock sweeping up above the recently thinned conifer forests. Further right, beyond Haystacks, are Buttermere and Crummock Water backed by the bulky fell of Grasmoor and the Derwent Fells. To the east, beyond Styhead Tarn, is the ridge linking Glaramara and Allen Crags, traversed earlier in the day.

Continuing north down gentle slopes you pass three small tarns in a shallow dip before a gentle climb up grassy slopes leads to the broad, rocky summit of Brandreth at 715m/2345 feet, from where you have a lovely view west down the Buttermere valley to its twin lakes. Heading north-east the path follows a wire fence across boggy terrain, passing a cluster of small tarns before reaching the rocky summits of Grey Knotts, the one on the right being the highest. Ahead is a very steep descent alongside a fence to the top of Honister Pass overlooked by the grassy shoulder of Dale Head and with the shapely Fleetwith Pike to the left.

The path ends at some slate trimming sheds and the car park behind Honister Hause Youth Hostel which stands on the site of the old mine manager's office. The still working Honister Mine, England's only remaining slate mine, is a reminder that green slate has been mined and quarried in this area since the seventeenth century. From the youth hostel, the old quarry road, now little more than a grass cart track in places, and running parallel with the main road, leads easily down to Seatoller.

INFORMATION

Start/Finish: Seatoller at the foot of Honister Pass, GR: 245138.

Distance: 17.7km/11 miles.

Walking Time/total climb: 6–8 hours/ 1455m (4774 feet).

Grading: Very Difficult; rugged walking on mainly good paths but with some steep rocky slopes.

Maps: OS Explorer OL4 & OL6 South-western area; Harvey Superwalker, Lakeland West.

Refreshments: Royal Oak Hotel, Rosthwaite.

Public Transport: Frequent bus service from Keswick to Seatoller.

Green and Great Gables from Brandreth.

Fleetwith Pike reflected in Crummock Water.

BUTTERMERE

After short journey from Borrowdale over the impressive Honister Pass with its slate quarries and mines, you enter the picturesque and narrow Buttermere valley. Here are green meadows, woodlands and charming hamlets, with the twin lakes of Buttermere and Crummock Water overlooked by hanging valleys and imposing hills; it is truly an unspoilt corner of Lakeland. One early writer caught the spirit of the place when he wrote:'That exquisite regard for proportion which nature has observed in the Lake District is nowhere more strikingly exemplified.'

The head of the valley is dominated by the shapely Fleetwith Pike and the craggy skyline of Haystacks.On the north-east side are the smooth, rounded slate hills of the Grasmoor and Derwent Fells, while to the south-west are the more rugged and craggy volcanic fells of the High Stile-High Crag range. It's all wonderful fell walking country and there are also some gentle lakeside walks. For fit walkers there is also the challenge of a full traverse of the valley skyline.

Birkness Combe and High Stile.

Situated on the B5289 road between Buttermere and Crummock Water is the charming village of Buttermere, an ideal centre for exploring the valley. The village lies on the flat, fertile area between the two lakes (which were originally one post-glacial lake). There are two pubs, the Bridge Inn and the Fish Inn, a youth hostel, a few B&Bs, a campsite and an outlying church, St James's, on a hillock above the village. In summer the Honister Rambler bus travels between Keswick and Buttermere. See also www.buttermere.co.uk.

Buttermere village became famous in the early nineteenth century by a story of an imposter, bigamist and fortune hunter named James Hatfield. He came to grief after falling in love and marrying the famed 'Maid of Buttermere' – Mary Robinson, daughter of the innkeeper of the Fish Inn. Melvyn Bragg retold the story of the famous beauty in 1984 in his book *The Maid of Buttermere*.

The Grasmoor fells across Crummock Water.

High Crag and Buttermere.

WALK 6 HIGH STILE IN BUTTERMERE

This classic Lakeland walk traverses the peaks around the south-western skyline of the Buttermere valley, crossing the wedge-shaped Fleetwith Pike, Haystacks and the craggy triumvirate of High Crag, High Stile and Red Pike. As a contrast to the earlier rocky terrain, the walk ends with a visit to Scale Force, Wordsworth's 'slender stream faintly illuminating a gloomy fissure,' followed by a gentle stroll along the wooded shoreline of Buttermere.

Gatesgarth to High Stile

From the car park opposite Gatesgarth Farm at the foot of Honister Pass, the day starts with an ascent of Fleetwith Pike's steep north-west ridge. The white cross at the base of the ridge commemorates Fanny Mercer, who fell to her death here in 1887. The ridge rises direct and uncompromising to the summit and as height is gained you get a splendid bird's-eye-view of Buttermere and Crummock Water hemmed in by the surrounding fells.

The Buttermere fells from Dale Head.

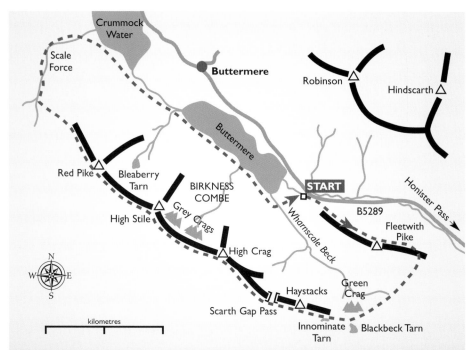

Robinson and Fleetwith Pike across Crummock Water.

Crossing Haystacks.

On a clear day one of the great attractions of Fleetwith Pike are the tremendous views from its lofty summit, ranging from Great Gable to Pillar. In the near distance, across the alluvial flats of Warnscale Bottom, lies the complex rocky terrain of Haystacks, and to its right the craggy hills of the High Stile range, with its fine ice-sculptured combes. During one particular ascent of Fleetwith Pike, I broke out of a sea of swirling mist into brilliant sunshine and clear skies to be greeted by a Brocken Spectre. Gradually three beautiful spectral-coloured haloes of a 'glory' formed around my dark shadow cast on the mists rising out of Warnscale Bottom; a memorable sight.

The top of Fleetwith Pike (648m/2126 feet) is merely the head of a spur at the end of a long summit ridge, which passes over the top of the impressive Honister Crag, with its quarried terraces and disused slate mine workings. From the crest of Honister Crag a path swings down right past Dubs Quarry – now more recently active – and past spoil heaps. A narrow descending track then traverses around the broad col and soggy area near Dubs Bottom, where Dubs Beck is crossed on route to the rocky knolls of Green Crag and the start of the crinkly undulations of Haystacks.

The craggy slopes of Birkness Combe.

This is a fascinating place with its complex array of small summits, rocky outcrops and shallow hollows, some of which contain pools and picturesque tarns, particularly Innominate and Blackbeck Tarns. A clear path works its way across the top of Haystacks but in misty conditions this can be a confusing area to walk.

However, on a calm, clear day one of the great sights along here is the view of Great Gable, the Scafells and the nearer cathedral-like buttresses of Pillar Rock reflected in Innominate Tarn. From the highest rocky top of Haystacks (597m/1959 feet), with its two cairns and tiny lake, an easy scramble down some small crags leads to a pitched path down to Scarth Gap. The pass was once a major trade route connecting Buttermere with Ennerdale, and then over Black Sail Pass to Wasdale and the coastal region.

Above: *A misty morning across Haystacks from Fleetwith Pike.*

Left: *Sunset over Buttermere and Crummock Water.*

Below: *A Brocken Spectre on Fleetwith Pike.*

High Crag seen from Haystacks.

Pillar reflected in Innominate Tarn, Haystacks.

In recent years a large amount of footpath restoration work has been carried out here, particularly the once-badly eroded scree slope leading up to Gamlin End. In 1997 National Trust workers constructed a superb pitched path here. The path climbs steeply up to the minor top of Seat then sharp zigzags lead up Gamlin End. The flat, grassy summit of High Crag (744m/2441 feet) is soon reached, where you can catch your breath and take in the view across to Great Gable at the head of Ennerdale.

Next is the start of the most exciting part of the walk — a 3km/2 mile switch-back ridge linking High Crag, High Stile and Red Pike. Enclosing the ridge to the north-east between High Crag and High Stile is Birkness Combe (sometimes spelt Burtness), the most impressive corner of Buttermere's fells and one of the most dramatic combes in Lakeland. Here are to be found the imposing Eagle Crag and the easier angled Grey Crag, whose slabby buttresses are now a popular venue for rock climbers. By contrast, the southern slopes are far less interesting. They are mainly grassy and fall steeply to the Ennerdale Forest.

High Stile to Gatesgarth

The path leads pleasantly round to High Stile (807m/2648 feet) whose actual summit is set a little towards Buttermere and provides excellent panoramic views with a fine array of peaks spread across the horizon. In misty weather, care is needed here to regain the crest path. The ridge now continues across the top of Chapel Crags, which overlook the rugged, scalloped hollow of Bleaberry Combe. From the edge of the escarpment you have a fine vantage point allowing impressive views down the gullies to the hanging valley with the dark pool of Bleaberry Tarn set in the massive amphitheatre between High Stile and Red Pike.

Standing at the top of Red Pike (755m/2477 feet), which often seems dwarfed by the surrounding hills, you can pick out five lakes — Buttermere, Derwent Water, Loweswater, Ennerdale Water and Crummock Water. The most direct way from the summit back to

Buttermere is to follow the obvious scarred, red granite scree slope down past the tarn, crossing the foaming Sourmilk Gill, the outlet from Bleaberry Tarn, and then to descend through the larches and pines of Burtness Wood to Buttermere's western tip.

However, a much more interesting end to the day is to continue north-west and follow a steep zigzag path down the red screes then contouring around the quiet and unfrequented Ling Comb. From here you can descend over heathery slopes to Scale Beck, which tumbles over the impressive waterfall of Scale Force. A steep path weaves its way down either side above the steep, tree-choked gorge to a footbridge at the base of the fall. At 47m/154 feet, this is the highest waterfall in Lakeland and in dry weather can be viewed by an easy scramble up to the main fall.

A stony track now leads right, traversing around a grassy spur overlooking Crummock Water before gently descending to join a path, which is followed right down to the shore-line. The walk ends with a pleasant stroll through Burtness Wood along the southern shore of Buttermere, then across tracks through pastureland back to Gatesgarth Farm.

INFORMATION

Start/Finish: Car park at the foot of Honister Pass, GR: 196150.
Distance: 16km/10 miles.
Walking Time/total climb: 6 hours/1050m (3445 feet).
Grading: Difficult; high level fell walking on mainly clear paths over high mountain ridges.
Maps: OS Explorer OL 4; Harvey Super Walker, Western Lakeland.
Refreshments: The Fish and Bridge Hotels and café in Buttermere village.
Public Transport: Very infrequent bus service from Keswick.

South-east from High Stile to the Scafell range.

53

WASDALE

Wasdale is arguably the most dramatic valley in the Lake District, a view reinforced as you drive from Nether Wasdale along the shore of Wast Water, England's deepest lake, its eastern shore overlooked by shattered buttresses, deep gullies and steep scree slopes plunging into the lake. But the most dramatic aspect is from Wasdale Head, the tiny settlement just beyond the lake at the end of the valley. Here in a great cirque are arranged some of the highest and most rugged mountains in England; the Scafell range, Great Gable, Kirkfell, Pillar, Red Pike and Yewbarrow.

There are numerous walks here to individual summits, around valley skylines, such as the classic Mosedale Horseshoe and, for fit walkers, there is the classic 27km/17 miles challenge of circumnavigating the full twisted skyline around Wasdale Head.

Accommodation is available at the National Trust campsite at Wasdale Head, the Wasdale Hall youth hostel at the foot of the western end of the lake, local B&Bs and the Wasdale Head Inn, one of the most celebrated of Lakeland hostelries. English rock climbing was born on these hills in the days when the inn's landlord – and champion liar – was Will Ritson (1808 – 1890). The Barn Door Shop next to the inn provides basic foodstuffs and outdoor gear, and there is camping in an adjacent field. Also at Wasdale Head is the church of St Olaf, supposedly England's smallest church, in whose graveyard are memorials to climbers, many who lost their lives on the surrounding fells.

Public transport is very limited in this area and if you don't fancy the long drive round to Wasdale then you can also approach these fells over high passes from Borrowdale or Buttermere. See also www.wasdaleweb.co.uk.

Above: *Climbers on The Napes, Great Gable.*
Below: *Storm over Scafell.*

Wasdale at dusk.

Wild camping on Scafell.

Wast Water screes.

55

Wasdale Head Inn.

WALK 7 PILLAR AND THE MOSEDALE HORSESHOE

One of Lakeland's classic ridge walks is the Mosedale Horseshoe. Mosedale is the remote northern offshoot of Wasdale Head and its craggy, undulating skyline contains some superb hills including Pillar, Steeple, Scoat Fell, Red Pike and the wedge-shaped hill of Yewbarrow. The walk is best done anticlockwise, leaving the very steep descent from Yewbarrow overlooking Wast Water until last.

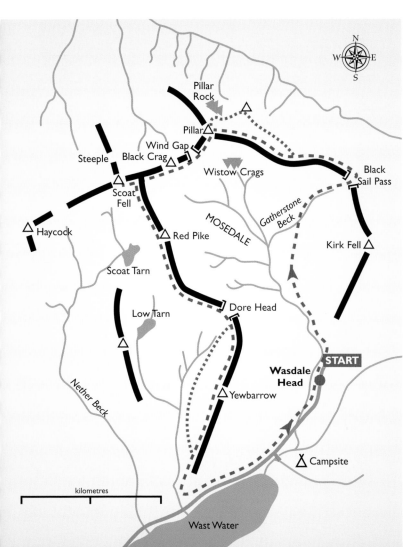

Although the impressive headwall of Mosedale is formed by Pillar, it is bulky Kirk Fell which dominates the entrance to the valley. To include Kirk Fell in the circuit depends not so much on whether you are a purist but whether you fancy attacking the soaring grassy tongue which falls directly from its twin-topped summit plateau almost to the hotel door at Wasdale Head. Experienced scramblers might want to ascend Kirk Fell via the classic Grade 3 route of Ill Gill which cleaves the south face. The choice is yours.

Wasdale Head to Pillar

From the Wasdale Head Inn a track leads alongside Mosedale Beck towards Kirk Fell (ignore the hump-backed footbridge over the beck) and climbs to a gate. Beyond here the track swings left around the foot of Kirk Fell from where you can take in the sweep of Mosedale. Initially easy walking, the path soon climbs towards Black Sail Pass, between Pillar and Kirk Fell. The path zigzags up the slopes, crossing Gatherstone Beck, from where Yewbarrow looks very impressive across the valley, before climbing steeply to the pass.

Mosedale.

Wistow Crags, a scrambler's way up Pillar.

Approaching Black Sail Pass.

Gatherstone Beck and Yewbarrow.

The High Level Route to Pillar Rock.

In the early stages of the walk, if you glance left into the heart of Mosedale you should be able to pick out a huge, two-stepped buttress rising above the grassy floor up the south-facing slopes of Pillar. These rocks are Wistow Crags whose crest provides an exciting 300m/985 feet Grade 3 scramble ending very close to the summit of Pillar. This is the quiet side of the mountain and you will often have the route to yourself.

Once you reach Sail Pass, the summit of Pillar can be approached left up the long grassy whaleback ridge via the minor top of Looking Stead or alternatively, and certainly more excitingly, along the High Level Route via Pillar Rock. From Looking Stead a narrow footpath contours through Hind and Green Coves and around rocky spurs overlooking the wooded slopes of Ennerdale to arrive at the prominent Robinson's Cairn. From here Pillar Rock with its cathedral-like buttresses looks magnificent.

Beyond Robinson Cairn the well-worn path continues across bouldery slopes up Pillar Cove to the Shamrock Traverse, a rocky scree-covered ramp set among dramatic rock scenery, although not quite as difficult as it might appear. Beyond the ramp, the path leads up to the neck behind Pillar Rock. The impressive crags are cut off from the hillside by the lesser summit of Pisgah, which in turn is separated from High Man – the actual top of Pillar Rock – by the cleft of Jordan Gap, putting the summit tantalisingly out of reach for most walkers. This is Lakeland's equivalent of the Inaccessible Pinnacle in the Cuillin Hills of Skye. It was from Pisgah that Moses viewed the Promised Land across the Jordan River – a great choice of names by Pillar's early explorers.

The usual way up High Man is via a Grade 3 scramble up the Slab and Notch, a popular and well-worn section of rock. First climbed way back in 1861 by the keeper of the St Bees lighthouse accompanied by four friends, the scramble demands respect and it has to be reversed unless you want a long abseil into Jordan Gap. Many will appreciate the security of a rope on this exposed outing, which is only for experienced scramblers.

Above, steep rocky slopes lead up towards the summit of Pillar and as height is gained you get a bird's-eye-view of Pillar Rock's craggy summit, which makes you realise just how rugged Pillar's flanks are, making it one of the roughest hills in Lakeland – and one which needs care in bad weather. Whichever approach is taken to the parade-ground summit of Pillar (892m/2927 feet), you get tremendous views. You can gaze across conifer-cloaked Ennerdale to the High Stile-High Crag range and beyond to the northern skyline stretching from Grasmoor to Skiddaw, while at the head of Ennerdale Great Gable stands aloof, backed by the Scafell range.

Robinson Cairn and Pillar Rock.

Approaching the top of Pillar from Pillar Rock.

High Man, Pillar Rock.

INFORMATION

Start/Finish: The Green, Wasdale Head, GR: 187084.

Distance: 17km/10.6 miles.

Walking Time/total climb: 6-7hours/1132m (3714 feet).

Grading: Very Difficult; a high level fell walk on good tracks and paths with some steep ascents and descents; an option of some easy scrambling. A serious route in winter conditions. Good navigation skills needed in poor visibility.

Maps: OS Explorer OL 4 and 6; Harvey Superwalker, Western Lakeland.

Refreshments: Wasdale Head Inn.

Public Transport: Train to Whitehaven for limited bus service to Gosforth with summer service only to Nether Wasdale.

Pillar to Wasdale Head

Descending rough slopes to the south-west, you arrive at the rocky notch of Wind Gap from where there are steep escape routes into both Ennerdale and Mosedale. Beyond Wind Gap the path crosses Black Crag and continues up to the broad, bouldery summit of Scoat Fell (841m/2759 feet) backed by the impressive cone of Steeple, with Ennerdale Water beyond. If time permits, a slight detour north-west to the small, shapely satellite peak of Steeple, surrounded on all sides by steep drops, is well worth the effort for the views into Ennerdale.

Back at Scoat Fell, gentle slopes now lead south-east down to a shallow col then across Red Pike (826m/2709 feet), a lofty vantage point for peering down its precipitous east face into Mosedale. The scene across to the broad summit plateau of Kirk Fell backed by the dome of Great Gable and the Scafells, high above the patchwork field patterns at Wasdale Head, is enchanting. After descending the skyline ridge over Red Pike in a general southerly direction, you arrive at Dore Head, with its tiny unnamed tarn overlooked by Yewbarrow's rearing Stirrup Crag.

Yewbarrow.

Kirkfell and Great Gable from Red Pike.

Sunset across Wast Water and The Screes.

Although the steep and dangerous Dore Head screes can be descended into Mosedale, an ascent of Yewbarrow is more in keeping with the rest of the walk. A short easy scramble up the rocks of Stirrup Crag leads to the grassy ridge of Yewbarrow, its high point at 628m/2060 feet, from where you can gaze across Wast Water to the Scafells. The descent of the rocky south ridge is very steep.

If the scramble up Stirrup Crag doesn't appeal, you can opt for an easier descent along a path which traverses the lower western slopes of Yewbarrow overlooking Over Beck. Both ways meet low down on the southern ridge from where steep, grassy slopes finally sweep down to Overbeck Bridge and Wast Water. The walk ends with a gentle stroll along the road back to Wasdale Head.

Great Gable at the head of Wasdale.

WALK 8 GREAT GABLE'S NEEDLE AND SPHINX

Great Gable's pyramid-shaped outline seen across Wast Water is one of the great views in the Lake District. The hill attracts walkers, climbers and scramblers like a magnet; even its name is something special – GREAT Gable. So evocative is its profile that the Lake District National Park selected the view of Gable from Wast Water as its emblem.

Sitting at the head of Wasdale, with Kirk Fell to its left beyond Beck Head, and Great End separated by Styhead Pass to its right, Great Gable dominates the view up the valley. From its rocky top, scree slopes plunge down the steep gullies of Little Hell Gate and Great Hell Gate either side of the series of narrow rocky ridges, known as the Napes. Situated at the foot of the ridges is the famous 24m (80 feet) high pinnacle of Napes Needle.

The easiest way up Great Gable from Wasdale Head is via the Styhead Pass, where a pitched path leads up steep rocky slopes to the summit. The walk described here is also via Styhead but it then sneaks off left to follow the Climbers' Traverse, a path which weaves a way across the foot of the Napes Ridges, offering a close up view of Napes Needle and Sphinx Rock. The traverse involves a small amount of easy scrambling (easily avoided by a lower path), and for more experienced scramblers, there are several challenging alternative ways. The return leg is via Beck Head.

Little Hell Gate and the Napes Ridges.

Above: *High on Sphinx Ridge.*

Left: *Great Gable towers above Wasdale Head.*

Below: *Field patterns at Wasdale Head.*

Above left: *Leaving the Dress Circle.*

Above right: *The Climbers' Traverse to Sphinx Rock.*

Below: *Napes Needle.*

Wasdale Head to Sphinx Rock

From The Green, near the Wasdale Head Inn, a walled track leads past the small church of St Olaf then through Burnthwaite Farm. Beyond the buildings, a grassy path crosses through the walled pastures overlooked by Kirkfell on the left, with Great Gable blocking the valley head. From here you can easily pick out Gable's knife-edge ridges and deep-cut scree gullies and, if you know where to look, Napes Needle. After crossing the footbridge over Gable Beck, the stony track eventually slants up across Gable's flank to Styhead Pass, the major gateway between Wasdale and Borrowdale.

The Climbers' Traverse starts up a path striking left across the fellside, eventually passing below the short outcrop of Kern Knotts with its two classic rock climbs of Kern Knotts Chimney and Innominate Crack. Beyond the outcrop the path rises steadily up to the steep slopes of red scree and boulders in Great Hell Gate, over-looked by the impressive buttress of Tophet Wall.

A short distance beyond the scree slope you get your first view of Napes Needle with the fan-like ridges of the Napes stacked in the background. Continuing below some rocks the path forks. The lower branch crosses easily to the next scree shoot of Little Hell Gate, while the more interesting right fork rises up a gully on the left-hand side of the famous Napes Needle for a closer look.

Countless numbers of climbers have ascended Napes Needle, many of them unaware of the significance of Walter Parry Haskett Smith's first daring solo climb in 1886. The event has been recognised as the probable birthplace of rock climbing as a distinct sport, rather than just training for mountaineering. Although the Needle is really the

domain of rock climbers, there is an excellent scramble which starts up the gully on the right, then crosses the gap between the pinnacle and Needle Ridge – an outing known as 'Threading the Needle'.

A short easy scramble up the gully to the left of Napes Needle lands you at a well-scratched rock ledge known as The Dress Circle, from where you can watch climbers tackling the Needle. On the skyline ahead you can now pick out the Sphinx Rock. Beyond The Dress Circle, the rocky traverse continues to a narrow squeeze through a crevasse behind an obvious large flake. Descending into the scree slope beyond the squeeze is the most awkward move on the traverse. Although only a short scrambling descent, care is needed here. Continuing along the stony path below a steep ridge, you quickly reach Sphinx Rock, its face-like profile staring stonily across to the Scafells.

Sphinx Rock overlooking Wasdale.

Heading for Styhead Pass from Wasdale.

65

Scrambling up Sphinx Ridge.

Great Hell Gate from the top of the Napes Ridges.

Sphinx Rock to Wasdale Head

For competent scramblers, Sphinx Ridge sweeping up above Sphinx Rock provides a superb way up to Westmorland's Crag and Gable's summit. Starting up an easy gully on the right of the Sphinx Rock, a series of rocky pinnacles and steps lead up to a narrow, Alpine-like crest where all the Napes Ridges converge below the broken rocks of Westmorland's Crag.

For non-scramblers the best way is to follow the path traversing below Sphinx Rock to Little Hell Gate, which is also reached via the easier lower path. A steep path now leads up the right-hand side of the screes towards the foot of Westmorland Crags. Alternatively you can scramble easily up the broken rocks of the conspicuous rocky pyramid of the White Napes, on the left-hand side of Little Hell Gate.

To reach the summit of Great Gable you head along a good path across a grassy neck up towards Westmorland's Crag, where the path sneaks up left over scree and shattered rocks to the top of the crag adorned by Westmorland's Cairn, a mere stone's throw south-west of the summit of Great Gable. The rugged top of Great Gable at 899m/2949 feet, with its uniformly steep slopes on all sides, gives a real feeling of space. From beside the huge cairn you have a great view down the full length of Wasdale with Wast Water reflecting the late afternoon sunshine, and also across central Lakeland.

Leaving the summit, the steep and rocky north-west slopes take you down to the grassy dip at Beck Head. If you want to extend the walk from here then a traverse over Kirk Fell returning via Black Sail Pass is highly recommended. Otherwise you head left and follow the steep path down the ridge of Gavel Neese to the valley floor, rejoining the path back to Wasdale Head. As you amble through the grassy meadows you can look back to Great Gable at the end of a scrambling adventure on a peak which has contributed so much to Lakeland's mountaineering history.

Above: *Westmorland's Crag.*

Below: *Great Gable and Wast Water.*

Descending Great Gable via Gavel Neese.

INFORMATION

Start/Finish: The Green near Wasdale Head Inn, GR: 187084.

Distance: 9.5km/6 miles.

Walking Time/total climb: 6 hours/842m (2762 feet).

Grading: Very Difficult; involves some craggy terrain and rocky ridges including some easy scrambling.

Maps: OS Explorer OL6; Harvey Superwalker, Lakeland West.

Refreshments: Wasdale Head Inn.

Public Transport: Train to Whitehaven for limited bus service to Gosforth with summer service only to Nether Wasdale.

Wast Water from the lower slopes of Lingmell.

WALK 9 SCAFELL PIKE VIA LINGMELL

Scafell Pike, England's highest mountain and the monarch of Lakeland fells, is the high point along a broad, rocky ridge stretching from Great End to the massive crag-girt Scafell. Lying at the centre of a hub of radiating valleys, there is an excellent choice of well-trodden approaches onto this high, rocky ridge. Of these, arguably the finest are from Wasdale Head, where there are several ways up Scafell Pike. The described circular walk offers a very pleasant and varied ascent via Lingmell, returning along the broad rocky ridge over Broad Crag to Great End, before descending to Wasdale Head via Styhead Pass.

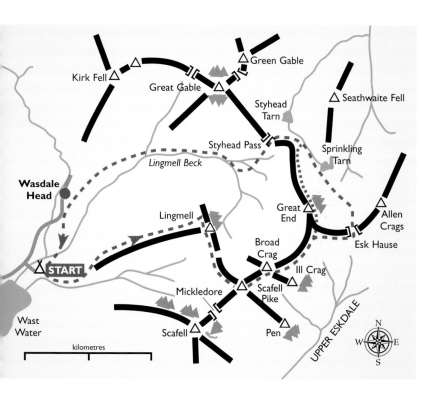

Wasdale Head to Scafell Pike

Starting from the car park at the National Trust campsite at Wasdale Head, a track leads towards Brackenclose, the Fell and Rock Climbing Club's hut. A path veers up left beside Lingmell Gill then forks left again up to the foot of a slender grassy ridge sweeping up to Lingmell. The path follows the crest, crossing an alternative approach path slanting up left from near The Green at Wasdale Head. As height is gained the view over Wast Water gradually opens up to the south-west.

The ridge rises steeply, eventually easing off at a broad grassy shoulder below Goat Crags. Across to the right, beyond the steep spur of Brown Tongue, stands Scafell, arguably the most spectacular mountain wall in Lakeland. One of the great sights of British mountain architecture is that of Scafell's west-facing cliffs turning blood red as the last rays of the setting sun pick out the features of this wild place in the very heart of Lakeland.

Lingmell and the Scafell range from Kirk Fell.

Scafell seen from Lingmell.

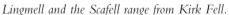

Beyond a ruined wall, grass and rocky slopes lead up past Goat Crags where you traverse left to reach Lingmell's north ridge crossing over several cairned tops and rocky steps to the summit at 807m/2648 feet. The elegant, slender cairn passed on one of the lower tiers has to be regularly re-built. Situated above the spectacular Lingmell Crag, which plummets down the north face to the chasm of Piers Gill, the top of Lingmell is a wonderful vantage point. From here you can contemplate Great Gable's Napes ridges, while to the south is a magnificent view of Scafell Pike, separated from its neighbour Scafell by the gap at Mickledore.

The west face of Scafell at dusk.

After descending south-east down a path over easy terrain to Lingmell Col, rocky slopes lead up to meet the Corridor Route, a popular way up Scafell Pike from Styhead Pass along a stony path slanting across the flanks of Broad Crag. The cairned path now weaves its way up rocky slopes to the north of Pikes Crag, arriving at a large cairn at the edge of the plateau. In misty weather this area can be very confusing. The well-worn stony path soon leads to the top of Scafell Pike, its summit at 978m/3210 feet easily identified by a huge walled platform cairn and an old trig point

Scafell Pike's summit.

off to one side and usually surrounded by hordes of walkers. It's rare to find this hallowed summit deserted for long.

The views from England's highest summit are superb, with an uninterrupted vista of Skiddaw to the north, the Helvellyn range to the east and the Consiton fells to the south. To the north-west the scene is dominated by the great bulk of Pillar and Great Gable.

Scafell Pike to Wasdale Head

From the summit, a stony path indicates the way north-east along the wide plateau ridge towards Broad Crag. The path descends steeply to the rocky gap of Broadcrag Col separating Little Narrowcove rising out of Eskdale on the right and Piers Gill on the left. Beyond the dip the path rises up to the rocky summit of Broad Crag (934m/3064 feet) with its mass of jumbled boulders making it one of the roughest summits in Lakeland. Just off the main path to the south-east is the isolated and rarely visited summit of Ill Crag (935m/3067 feet), worth a slight detour just for the stunning views into Upper Eskdale.

Great Gable seen from Scafell Pike.

Lingmell provides a great view of Great Gable.

Lingmell and the Scafells across Wast Water.

Continuing north, the main path leads towards the fine rocky dome of the outlying peak of Great End (910m/2985 feet), a much-neglected summit. At a depression the main path veers right down Calf Cove. If you want to visit Great End, continue along a path which climbs easily up to its twin summits. Great End's north-east face, with its prominent crags and gullies, comes into its own in winter, providing some popular snow and ice climbs. Great End's steep north ridge can be descended via The Band and is not as intimidating as it looks, although it is rocky and requires care. The ridge eventually lands you at Seathwaite Fell just below Sprinkling Tarn.

If this way looks too intimidating, you can head back south to the dip and follow the main path which descends below Great End's eastern scree slopes to the wide plateau of Esk Hause, one of the major cross-roads in the area, linking Wasdale, Eskdale, Langdale and Borrowdale. From Esk Hause a good 'highway' leads north-west under Great End's dramatic cliffs and past the shaley ravine of Ruddy Gill. The path skirts the southern shore of Sprinkling Tarn and continues down towards Styhead Tarn before veering left to the usually busy Styhead Pass overlooked by the frowning dome of Great Gable.

Although the worn path to Wasdale Head can now be followed left as it slants down across Great Gable's flanks, a more interesting and quieter alternative, is to descend a grassy path alongside Lingmell Beck, which passes through lovely surroundings overlooked on the left by the craggy slopes of Lingmell. The path on the north side of the gill eventually bears off right through bracken to meet the main path descending from Styhead Pass.

The path crosses through walled pastures to Burnthwaite Farm, where a walled farm track leads past the church of St Olaf to The Green just beyond the Wasdale Head Inn. If you started at the NT car park, head along the road for a short distance and take a signed field path to the left, passing through areas of scrub and crossing Lingmell Beck back to the campsite and car park.

INFORMATION

Start/Finish: Car park at the NT campsite near Brackenclose, GR: 182076 or The Green near Wasdale Head Inn, GR: 187084.
Distance: 13km/8 miles.
Walking Time/total climb: 6-8 hours/ 1086m (3563 feet).
Grading: Very Difficult; a serious high level walk on mainly good paths and some craggy terrain - best attempted during a spell of clear, dry weather. Good navigation skills essential.
Maps: OS Explorer OL 6; Harvey Superwalker, Lakeland West.
Refreshments: Wasdale Head Inn.
Public Transport: Train to Whitehaven for limited bus service to Gosforth with summer service only to Nether Wasdale.

Scafell Pike from Pen.

The Scafell range from Harter Fell.

ESKDALE

Eskdale is usually approached by an exciting drive over the Hardknott and Wrynose Passes or a lengthy detour around the coast, guaranteeing the isolation of this beautiful valley. Despite it having no lake, the valley is a place of contrasts. Gentle fells roll down to the sea and sand dunes at its exit at Ravenglass, while in its lower section there are oak woodlands, wonderful river scenery and hidden waterfalls. At the foot of Hardknott Pass, the dale swings north up to the mountain sanctuary of Upper Eskdale, buttressed by some of the steepest and rockiest slopes in Lakeland.

The valley has had an important route through it since Roman times when a road connected the fort of *Glannaventa* (Ravenglass) with the forts of *Mediobogdum* (Hardknott Fort) and *Galava* (Ambleside). Iron ore has been extracted here since Roman times and in 1875, the narrow gauge steam railway known affectionately as 'La'al Ratty' (Little Ratty) following the River Esk was built to carry ore from the mines to the coast. Nowadays the miniature steam and diesel trains of the celebrated Ravenglass and Eskdale Railway link with the Cumbria Coast Line and transport walkers and tourists alike from Ravenglass to Dalegarth, near Boot. Accommodation in the valley is provided at hotels, B&Bs, Eskdale youth hostel and several campsites.

Though the hills surrounding the valley head are shared with Langdale and Wasdale, they form one of the most impressive rims of any Lakeland valley, and provide some superb high level walks and rocky scrambles on England's highest fells. Fit walkers might wish to tackle the full Eskdale skyline, with over 2015m/6610 feet of ascent during the 27km/16.7 miles circuit. In marked contrast, sweeping south from Eskdale is an area of open moorland and knobbly fells linking the shapely peak of Harter Fell with the Ulpha and Birker Fells. Here you can often walk for miles and see few other people. Apart from high level walks there are also easy riverside strolls for when the tops are out of condition.

Looking north across Eskdale to Slight Side.

Upper Eskdale from near Hardknott Fort.

WALK 10 ALONG THE SCAFELL CREST

This classic and demanding walk starts at Brotherilkeld at the foot of Hardknott Pass and enters the hidden wilderness of Upper Eskdale. The extra effort required to reach this sanctuary makes an ascent of Scafell Pike via the isolated summit of Pen, or Little Narrow Cove, all the more special. There are also several options for experienced scramblers, for here are to be found the longest ridge and buttress approaches to the Scafells. After crossing from Scafell Pike to Scafell, the return leg is down the easy wide grassy spur of Slight Side.

Brotherilkeld to Scafell Pike

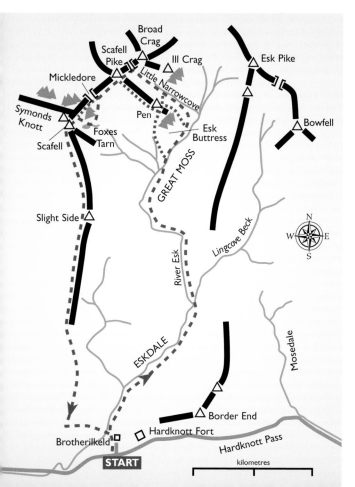

From the farmhouse at Brotherilkeld, a good path hugs the south side of the river and passes through pastures. Just beyond where the River Esk is joined by Lingcove Beck at Throstle Garth, the path forks left across a single-arched packhorse bridge, then heads up bracken covered slopes, skirting Esk Gorge, a beautiful spot below Green Crag. The path finally enters the basin of Great Moss, the site of a shallow lake scoured out during the last Ice Age. Above the boggy terrain, scree and broken rocky slopes sweep up to the Scafell summits. On the left-hand side of this spectacular amphitheatre are the shattered cliffs of Cam Spout, a rugged spur of Scafell with its famous waterfalls to the right and a popular walkers' path to the skyline notch at Mickledore.

A little further up the valley, beyond Cam Spout, stands the steep, prow-like pillar of Esk Buttress, named Dow Crag on maps. Above the crag is the isolated cone of Pen, Scafell Pike's isolated satellite peak which offers a gem of an approach route to the tops where you will rarely meet other people. Between Esk Buttress and the shattered cliffs of Ill Crag to the right, is the scree gully of Little Narrowcove, which also gives a secluded ascent to Scafell Pike. Beyond Ill Crag's broken cliffs the path rises to Esk Hause, a major cross-roads of paths and an easier gateway to the Scafell ridge.

Scafell Pike, Pen and Ill Crag across Great Moss.

The Scafell range from Border End.

Esk Buttress.

Upper Eskdale with Bowfell seen ahead.

Scafell Pike via Pen

Esk Buttress is bounded on its right-hand side by Thor's Buttress which, for competent scramblers, provides a great approach to the summit of Pen. This Grade 3 route ascends easy angled rocks left of the conspicuous dark slash of Thor's Cave, above which ledges and exposed rough slabs provide some fine scrambling. The buttress eventually merges into the hillside where easy slopes lead up to Pen's small summit cone with its fine views across Upper Eskdale. Pen is connected to Scafell Pike by a broad and straightforward rocky ridge, ending abruptly just a short distance from the top of Scafell Pike. For non-scramblers, the top of Pen can be reached via steep slopes on the left-hand side of Esk Buttress and also along a narrow path from Little Narrowcove.

Scafell Pike via Little Narrowcove

For walkers an equally fine way up Scafell Pike is via Little Narrowcove. The way into the cove starts at a large cairn beside the infant River Esk from where a path slants up the hillside into the secretive confines of Little Narrowcove. The upper section consists of a zigzag path up steep scree slopes to suddenly arrive at Broadcrag col. Scafell Pike's summit (978m/3210 feet) is just a short distance up to the left, its top crowned by a huge circular rocky platform. Despite the drabness of the plateau, the panoramic views are superb.

Above left: *Bowfell and Esk Pike from Pen.*

Above right: *Ill Crag seen across Little Narrowcove from Pen.*

Below: *Balancing up Thor's Buttress, Pen.*

Pike's Crag at dusk.

Scafell Pike to Scafell

Leaving the summit, a cairned path leads south-west down boulder-strewn slopes to the narrow, red scree and grassy crest of Mickledore, which ends abruptly at the steep cliffs defending the northern flank of Scafell. The beetling East Buttress of Scafell overlooking Eskdale and the impressive cliffs of Scafell Crag on the Wasdale side are redolent with the history of Lakeland rock climbing. In fact more than any other peak in Lakeland, Scafell is a climbers' mountain.

For competent scramblers there is only one route from Mickledore and that is Broad Stand which breaches Scafell's craggy defences at their lowest point. The first reputed descent of this 'bad step', and the first recorded rock climb in Britain, was made by Wordsworth's friend the poet, Samuel Taylor Coleridge on 8 August, 1802. He had an epic trip and managed to safely negotiate this rocky impasse by lowering himself from his hands and then letting himself drop onto a sloping ledge, his 'limbs all in a tremble.'

Although Broad Stand is the normal descent route for rock climbers, it's still a challenge for scramblers and has gained a certain notoriety among hill-goers. The route starts a short distance down the Eskdale side at a tight squeeze through a deep, polished cleft – a 'fat man's agony' – followed by an exposed traverse left onto a sloping platform below an overhanging corner. Despite having only scrambled a short distance up the rocks, the exposure pulls at your heels, as the scree slope drops away rapidly to the left. A slip would have disastrous consequences, and the security of a rope here is very comforting. The corner is overcome by steep moves on good, though smooth, holds on its left-hand wall. Above, a series of easy ledges and scree-strewn slabs lead up to the rocky summit ridge. If in any doubt about Broad Stand, opt for the Foxes Tarn route instead.

The Foxes Tarn approach is really the only safe way to outflank the precipices. This involves a long detour left down scree slopes below the overhanging cliffs of the East

A mist-filled Wasdale at dusk seen from Scafell.

Mickledore and crag-girted Scafell.

INFORMATION

Start/Finish: Brotherilkeld; roadside pull off at GR: 210011.

Distance: 16km/10 miles.

Walking Time/total climb: 6-8 hours/ 1162m (3812 feet).

Grading: Very Difficult; this is the most serious and demanding circuit in the book and passes through some very craggy terrain. This outing should only be undertaken by those with good hill-walking skills and experience. If you opt for the scrambling alternatives, basic rock climbing skills are essential.

Maps: OS Explorer OL6; Harvey Superwalker, Lakeland West.

Refreshments: Woolpack Inn, near Boot, Eskdale.

Public Transport: Rail service to Ravenglass then narrow gauge railway to Eskdale.

Buttress and then re-ascending up a rocky path through a gully to Foxes Tarn – 'a dark jewel in a wild setting.' From the small tarn, a pitched path zigzags steeply up to a shallow dip with the summit of Scafell about 50m/55 yards to the south. The other route to the summit is via the classic Lord's Rake, which outflanks the steep cliffs of Scafell Crag on the right-hand side, with the West Wall Traverse leading to a steep finish up Deep Gill. Sadly, at the present time (2006) this approach is not recommended due to recent rock falls and slippages, which have left the route in a dangerous condition.

From the top of the Foxes Tarn path a short walk right leads to a grassy area at the top of Deep Gill, overlooked by the prominent and accessible rocky knoll of Symond's Knott. Framed by the rocks of Symond's Knott and the craggy Scafell Pinnacle there is a lovely view to Great Gable and the Pillar Group. A short walk past the Pinnacle provides a splendid view down to Pike's Crag and beyond to Scafell Pike. Heading back south, the top of Scafell (964m/3162 feet) is soon reached and is a place to linger to appreciate the broad seaward view of Morcambe Bay and the Duddon and Ravenglass Estuaries.

North across Eskdale to Slight Side.

The summit of Scafell.

Scafell Pinnacle backed by the Pillar Fells.

Scafell to Brotherilkeld

Although Scafell has impressive defences on its northern side, there are easier descents south along a steep ridge over the rocky top of Slight Side. During the upper section of the descent you get an unusual perspective of Pen, which now stands out proudly as an isolated, pointed peak in a soaring wilderness of craggy slopes.

The footpath continues south down the broad grassy ridge to Taw House Farm then across the footbridge over the Esk to Brotherilkeld Farm and the end of a magnificent mountain day.

Scafell and Mickledore from the east.

Harter Fell's west ridge.

WALK 11 EXPLORING HARTER AND ULPHA FELLS

Many walkers who come to Eskdale have their sights set on an ascent of Scafell or Harter Fell. Few of them venture across the open moors which sweep south from Eskdale and enclosed by the Duddon valley to the east and the Ulpha to Eskdale road to the west. Yet this rocky moorland terrain including the Harter, Ulpha and Birker Fells, with the principal summits of Harter Fell, Crook Crag, Green Crag and Great Worm Crag, provides some excellent walking with many hidden corners to be discovered.

This circular walk through the wild moorland landscape starts and finishes at the Woolpack Inn in Eskdale, and includes a visit to Stanley Force, one of Lakeland's most charming waterfalls. An ascent of Harter Fell is the highlight of the walk and although this craggy cone-shaped peak is not very high, its perfectly proportioned shape set in a stunning position makes it very attractive.

The Woolpack Inn to Green Crag

About 180m/200 yards along the road west of the Woolpack Inn, a lane leads left for Penny Hill Farm, crossing the River Esk at Doctor Bridge. Originally a packhorse bridge it was widened in the early eighteenth century by Dr Edward Tyson, hence the name. Beyond the bridge you turn immediately left along the track to Penny Hill Farm beyond which the path climbs right up the hillside above the wooded banks of the River Esk towards the foot of Harter Fell's west ridge. The path weaves its way up the ridge and as height is steadily gained, the views of lower Eskdale, with its farm buildings and walled green fields overlooked by bracken-covered fells, looks quite pastoral.

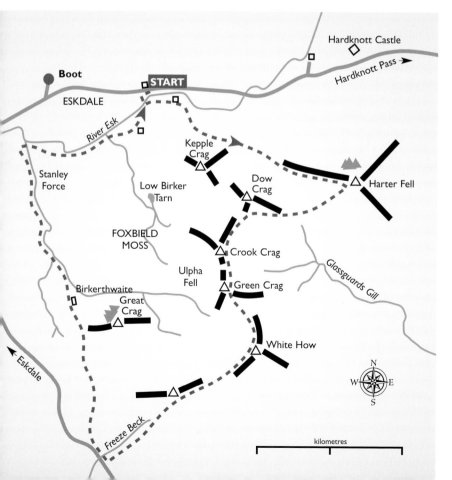

The Scafell range from Harter Fell.

The summit of Harter Fell.

Continuing up the twisting path around grassy and rocky knolls you finally arrive at a grassy platform at the summit surrounded by outcrops of rock. There are three actual summits; one is a trig point on top of a rocky outcrop which is not the highest point; that is on one of the twin-rocky tops a few yards to the east at 653m/2142 feet. Both rocky summits are reached by short, easy scrambles.

Straddling the top end of the Eskdale and the Duddon valley, Harter Fell's rocky top is one of the best viewpoints in the area, especially north-west into the heart of Upper Eskdale, a dramatic amphitheatre surrounded by rugged hills. To the east, beyond the Dunnerdale Forest, and looking remarkably close, is the Coniston range. One of the most unusual perspectives is a bird's-eye-view of the walled ruins of the Roman fort of Hardknott Castle, at the foot of Hardknott Pass.

You also get a good view west to the next stage of the walk across a vast stretch of grass and heather moorland dotted with rocky knolls and craggy summits. From the summit, a steep path drops south-west to the edge of a forest on a broad grassy pass. The path coming in on the left ascends through the woods from the beauty spot at Birks Bridge in the Duddon valley.

Looking north-east from Crook Crag to Harter Fell.

Approaching the top of Green Crag.

The high point of Harter Fell.

North from Green Crag to the Scafell range.

Continuing west across the broad grassy pass, which is often boggy after rain, heather and grassy slopes lead up to the conspicuous dip between Crook Crag and Kepple Crag. Turning left at the dip, a faint path weaves a way up though thick heather and bilberry, passing rocky outcrops dotted along a broad, undulating ridge leading up towards the rocky summit of Crook Crag. This can be a very confusing area in misty weather. A short easy scramble up some slabs and rocky steps leads to the summit cairn of Crook Crag, which stands on the western end of a long rocky ridge.

Beyond Crook Crag, the path continues through heather up to The Pike, a conical-shaped rocky protuberance, whose top is easily reached by a short scramble up a series of steps. Returning to the path it now crosses a grassy col, before swinging right and ascending steep grassy slopes to the foot of the summit tower of Green Crag. Here, a faint path follows a natural grassy shelf slanting up right then up bouldery slopes to the summit of Green Crag, its high point being a cairn on top of rocky outcrop at 489m/1604 feet. This is another fine viewpoint especially looking back to The Pike, backed by the shapely summit of Harter Fell. Down to the west is the great boggy hollow of Foxbield Moss with Low Birker Tarn in a hollow overlooked by Tarn Crag.

Green Crag to the Woolpack Inn

Continuing south-east along another broad grassy ridge dotted with yet more rocky knolls you arrive at White How, a rock table marking its top. Swinging south-west, the grassy dome of Great Worm Crag is crossed before descending rough fell grass, skirting Rough Crag on its eastern flank. Bearing left through a boggy section, Freeze Beck is followed down to meet the Eskdale to Ulpha road about 200m/220 yards north-west of the Winds Gate cattle grid.

Turning right along the road for about 350m/380 yards, a clear path branches north across heather moorland towards Birkerthwaite Farm, overlooked to the east by the commanding Great Crag. At the farm, a track is joined leading past cottages at Low Ground and on to the head of Stanley

Force, also known as Dalegarth Force since it was named after the Stanleys who once lived at nearby Dalegarth Hall.

The terrain underfoot changes dramatically now as waterfalls and wooded ravines replace moors and crags. A good path drops down the banks of the ravine to a bridge over the river, from where you can make a short diversion back up the ravine for a closer look at the main falls. This is a spectacular setting with the river tumbling into a narrow, rocky gorge overhung by trees. Returning to the bridge, the path continues down through woods until you come to a bridge. Across the bridge a bridleway takes you along the southern banks of the River Esk, passing Low Birker Farm to rejoin the outward route at Doctor Bridge.

INFORMATION

Start/Finish: Woolpack Inn, near Boot, GR:190010.
Distance: 17km/10.5 miles.
Walking Time/total climb: 6 hours/813m (2667 feet).
Grading: Moderate; rough moorland and craggy terrain with clear paths at low level and faint paths along the tops. Good navigation skills needed in misty conditions; some easy scrambling and boggy terrain.
Maps: OS Explorer OL 6; Harvey Superwalker, Lakeland South West.
Refreshments: The Woolpack Inn and The Burnmoor Inn, Boot
Public Transport: Railway service to Ravenglass for the Eskdale Railway.

Green Crag seen across Foxbield Moss.

Scrambling up Harrison Stickle backed by Pavey Ark.

A winter crossing of Crinkle Crags.

LANGDALE

Langdale (from the Norse meaning 'long valley'), cuts deep into the south-eastern corner of the Western Fells. Heading west from Ambleside, the valley is wide and overlooked by low wooded hills. You then pass through the hamlets of Skelwith Bridge, Elterwater and Chapel Stile, beyond which you emerge into the wide curve of Great Langdale, gateway to a range of rugged fells surrounding the head of the valley.

Here the dale divides into the craggy recesses of Oxendale and Mickleden, overlooked by Pike o'Blisco, the Crinkles and Bowfell, with the rocky group of Pike o'Stickle, Harrison Stickle and Pavey Ark – the Langdale Pikes – being the centrepiece and most familiar to visitors. The valley is also one of the oldest industrialised parts of the area, evidenced by a Stone Age axe 'factory' on the slopes below the Langdale Pikes.

The craggy fells around the head of Great Langdale offer some wonderful walks through dramatic surroundings and, not surprisingly, the valley is very popular with tourists, walkers, scramblers and rock climbers. For fit walkers the long skyline horse-shoe around the head of the valley gives a 26km/16miles challenging and classic outing, one of Lakeland's best.

Because of its ease of access, the valley car parks are often very crowded at peak times. However, a regular 'Langdale Rambler' bus service links Ambleside with the Old and New Dungeon Ghyll Hotels at the valley head. There is plenty of accommodation in the valley including hotels, B&Bs, the National Trust campsite and youth hostels at Elterwater and Loughrigg. See also www.langdaleweb.co.uk

The classic view of the Langdale Pikes across Blea Tarn.

Oxendale from Lingmoor Fell.

WALK 12 AN OXENDALE OUTING

Oxendale, at the head of the Langdale valley, is a wild and rugged place, its slopes cut by deep ravines below a craggy skyline stretching from Pike o'Blisco to Crinkle Crags and Bowfell. Brown Gill, along with Crinkle Gill and Hell Gill, form deep clefts above Oxendale, and are among the most impressive in the area, especially after prolonged heavy rain when they create a spectacular sight as they enter the Oxendale River quite close together.

Starting from the Old Dungeon Ghyll Hotel this excellent and varied outing around Oxendale's skyline gives a challenging traverse over craggy terrain which is never really difficult but still requires care on some of the steeper sections. Throughout the walk the views are superb. The return leg is via Esk Hause and through the much gentler valley floor of Mickleden.

Walkers approaching Red Tarn.

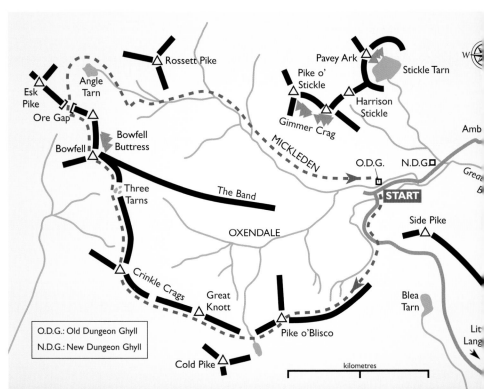

The Old Dungeon Ghyll to Bowfell

Beyond the Old Dungeon Ghyll Hotel the narrow road leads to Wall End Farm from where the full sweep of the fells, cut into by Oxendale, are seen to good effect. Leaving the road at the hairpins above the farm, a constructed path climbs steeply over bracken-covered slopes and outcrops of pinkish rock up the left-hand side of Redacre Gill.

After the steep initial section a cairned, pitched path climbs steadily up to the shoulder of Wrynose Fell before swinging right to reach the final slopes where a bit of scrambling lands you at the rocky, belvedere summit of Pike o'Blisco (705m/2313 feet). From the twin summits you can look down into Oxendale and across to Crinkle Crags, backed by Bowfell, now seen in true perspective. Across the jigsaw-patterned valley fields the Langdale Pikes are clearly defined and look almost close enough to touch.

Some of the hard-gained height is now lost as you descend a good path south-west to a grassy saddle and the waters of Red Tarn. This pass is an important cross-roads where several paths converge near the outlet of the tarn. The route from Wrynose passes this way and continues down rocky Brown Gill to Oxendale, a good escape route in bad weather and at one time probably used by packhorse trains in the heyday of ore-mining in the area.

The Band and Bowfell.

Heading up Pike o'Blisco.

89

The final rocky steps to the top of Pike o'Blisco.

Crinkle Crags and Bowfell reflected in Red Tarn.

Ahead now lies the Crinkles, which are easily approached up a path on the northern flanks of Cold Pike. Seen from the Langdale valley the aptly-named Crinkle Crags appear as a serrated skyline but on closer acquaintance, turn out to be a series of undulating, rocky buttresses separated by scree gullies above steep, grassy slopes; a bit reminiscent of Haystacks. The traverse of the five summits is exhilarating, with unsurpassed views of the Coniston Hills, the Duddon valley, Eskdale, the Scafell range, Bowfell and the Langdale Pikes.

Above left: *A snowy Bowfell summit.*
Above right: *Snow storm on the Crinkles.*

From the top of the first pinnacle you get a grandstand view across Great Cove to the rocky dome of the second top with its infamous 'bad step' forming the only awkward section along the ridge. The obstacle is bypassed by a short, polished climb up the right wall of a scree gully jammed by a huge boulder. If this approach does not appeal then a detour can be made from the col up a cairned path to the left which lands you on the ridge just west of the main summit.

Above the 'bad step' it is easy to pick a way up a rocky path to the summit of the second, and highest, of the Crinkles, named Long Top (859m/2818 feet). This summit ridge runs at right angles to the main knobbly spine and in misty conditions can be an awkward place to negotiate. Once the shoulder of Shelter Crags is crossed, broken slopes and scree are descended to the shallow depression at Three Tarns over-looked by Bowfell, its Eskdale face split by the crumbling scree gullies known as Bowfell Links. This broad col is the most direct way from Langdale into Eskdale and in ancient times it was an important trade route to the coast.

Descending to Ore Gap.

Beyond the pass, an obvious rocky path leads tediously up the long south ridge of Bowfell, eventually crossing a boulder field to arrive at the summit cairn at 902m/2959 feet situated on top of a large rock outcrop on the western side of the upper plateau. Bowfell is a beautiful conical peak that has commanding views into Eskdale, Langdale and Langstrath and ranks as one of Lakeland's finest summits. This is a great place to enjoy the panorama, especially the rugged outline of the Scafell range across Upper Eskdale.

Bowfell to the Old Dungeon Ghyll

Leaving the summit, a line of cairns points the way north where a detour can be made across rough ground to Bowfell's northern top (866m/2841 feet) where Great Gable comes into view beyond Great End. Many walkers visiting the top of Bowfell are oblivious to the delights to be found on its north-estern face overlooking Mickleden. Here is the huge area of tilted slabs known as the Great Slab, but it is the cathedral-like Bowfell Buttress which holds pride of place for climbers.

The Old Dungeon Ghyll overlooked by Loft Crag.

The main path now leaves Bowfell and crosses rocks and boulders before swinging west down to the brown, iron-stained rocks of Ore Gap. From here, easy slopes lead up to Esk Pike, its rocky summit at 885m/2904 feet, looking quite insignificant among the surrounding rugged hills. By following a rocky path down its north-west ridge you soon arrive at the saddle of Esk Hause, a major crossing point of footpaths. A short distance to the north-east lies the main highway into Langdale, which is followed east down past Angle Tarn and the steep path by Rossett Gill.

The walk ends with a pleasant stroll back to the Old Dungeon Ghyll Hotel along the broad path through Mickleden, from whose green meadows the lengthening shadows on the frowning Crinkles can be seen high above Oxendale.

INFORMATION

Start/Finish: Car park by the Old Dungeon Ghyll Hotel, GR: 286061.
Distance: 16km/10 miles.
Walking Time/total climb: 6 hours/1288m (4225 feet).
Grading: Very Difficult; rough fell walking with a lot of steep rocky slopes and occasional scrambling; care needed in mist.
Maps: OS Explorer OL 6; Harvey Superwalker Lakeland West and Central.
Refreshments: New and Old Dungeon Ghyll Hotels; The Wainwright Inn, Chapel Stile.
Public Transport: Langdale Rambler bus from Ambleside.

The Scafell range seen from Bowfell.

The Langdale Pikes from Lingmoor Fell.

WALK 13   A LANGDALE JAUNT

The familiar jagged profile of the Langdale Pikes seen reflected at dawn in the calm waters of Blea Tarn (Wordsworth's 'liquid pool that glittered in the sun') or Elterwater, are among the favourite views of the Lake District. It is these classic post-card pictures which have contributed to making the very accessible Greater Langdale so popular.

For walkers, scramblers and rock climbers, it is the craggy fells of the Langdale Pikes, including Harrison Stickle, Pike o'Stickle and Pavey Ark, which are the most appealing. This relatively short, but classic circuit, starting at the New Dungeon Ghyll Hotel, tackles the Langdale Pikes including, if so inclined, the easy scramble up Jack's Rake. The return leg is via Stake Pass and Mickleden.

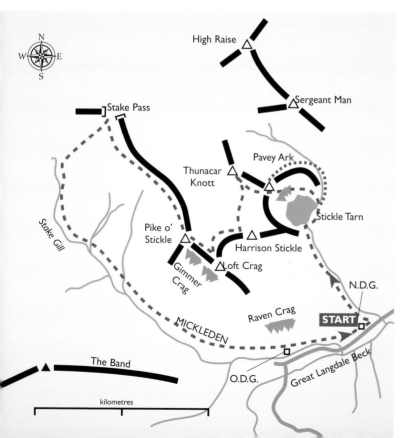

New Dungeon Ghyll to Pavey Ark

A path from the National Trust car park leads between Sticklebarn Tavern and the New Dungeon Ghyll Hotel. Beyond a field the path forks and the right-hand branch is taken across a wooden footbridge from where the right bank of Mill Gill (more commonly known as Stickle Ghyll), which flows from Stickle Tarn is followed. From the pitched path you can peer into the gill where a series of cascades tumble down the rocky gorge. In its upper section the path climbs steeply up the left-hand side of the gill, eventually ascending over some rocky formations to level off at Stickle Tarn backed by the beetling cliffs of Pavey Ark.

An obvious ascending runnel slanting from right to left across Pavey Ark's huge, bow-shaped grey crags is Jack's Rake, a Grade 1 scramble. Although not difficult or exposed, it does pass through some tremendous rock scenery to provide one of Lakeland's most

Left: *An autumn day in Langdale.*

Above: *Pavey Ark and Jack's Rake.*

Below: *Scrambling up the trench of Jack's Rake.*

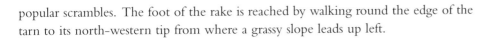

popular scrambles. The foot of the rake is reached by walking round the edge of the tarn to its north-western tip from where a grassy slope leads up left.

The main difficulties lie in the upper section where a series of short, polished walls can often be confusing, especially in wet and misty weather. Experienced and adventurous scramblers will relish this part and probably end Jack's Rake by tackling the summit tower direct up its left edge on superb rock in an exposed position high above Stickle Tarn. From the rake you get a bird's-eye-view of Stickle Tarn and can look across to Harrison Stickle whose east ridge forms a prominent stepped skyline. From the top of Jack's Rake, a series of paths lead across past several rocky hummocks to the summit cairn of Pavey Ark (700m/2297 feet), situated on a rocky outcrop beyond a derelict wall.

The final section of Jack's Rake above Stickle Tarn.

Harrison Stickle from Jack's Rake.

If Jack's Rake is crowded, or you fancy an easier scramble, then you could ascend Easy Gully, the obvious gully cutting up to the right of Jack's Rake. There are some awkward boulders to negotiate at the top before the steep slope of North Rake is joined, which is followed up to the left. However, for walkers, the easiest way is to head along the east shore of the lake and follow a path, which rises alongside Bright Beck. The path then swings left across the beck and climbs steeply up North Rake, sheltered on either side by crags. About half way up the rake, the path from Easy Gully comes in from the left. Where the path emerges at the top of North Rake, you turn left and head along paths to the summit of Pavey Ark where you can enjoy stunning panoramic views, especially across the head of Great Langdale to Bowfell and the Scafells.

Harrison Stickle from Side Pike.

Pavey Ark to the New Dungeon Ghyll

Pavey Ark is really an outlying crag of Thunacar Knott, whose grassy summit dome with a small cairn at 723m/2372 feet is easily reached along a cairned path to the west, past some small tarns. Skiddaw and the Derwent Fells look great from here. A grassy path now descends gently south before a short climb up the northern flank of Harrison Stickle.

If you opted out of the walk across from Pavey Ark to Thunacar Knott, then you can follow a path south, skirting around the rim of the Stickle Tarn basin before climbing up to the summit cairn of Harrison Stickle (736m/2414 feet). From its rocky top, the cliffs of Pavey Ark look quite intimidating.

Pavey Ark from Harrison Stickle.

Climbers on Raven Crag.

Leaving behind Harrison Stickle, the conspicuous sugar-loaf top of Pike o'Stickle beckons beyond the great ravine of Dungeon Ghyll and across the squelchy grass of Harrison Combe. The infant beck soon matures as it rushes its way over a series of dramatic falls down Dungeon Ghyll into Langdale. Instead of making a bee-line for Pike o'Stickle, it's worth making a slight detour left to Loft Crag with its spectacular cliffs of Gimmer Crag, where are to be found some of Lakeland's best climbing on impeccable rock. Here is the sensational climb of Kipling's Groove, apparently so-named because it's 'ruddy hard!'.

Below left: *The thimble-shaped Pike o'Stickle.*

Below right: *Martcrag Moor leading down to Stake Pass.*

Heading back north, Pike o'Stickle's unusual dome of rock is soon reached where you need to use your hands as well as feet to reach its rounded summit at 709m/2326 feet. At the foot of a scree-choked gully to the east of the Pike is an important archaeological site where a stone-axe factory flourished in the Neolithic and Early Bronze Ages. A hard band of porcellanite running across the slope provided the hard-wearing material for the axes. The crude axe heads were polished elsewhere and have turned up in countries such as France.

INFORMATION

Start/Finish: Car parks at the New Dungeon Ghyll Hotel, GR: 294064.
Distance: 13km/8 miles.
Walking Time/total climb: 5 hours/700m (2300 feet).
Grading: Difficult; some steep ascents and descents on mainly good paths with the option of some Grade 1 scrambling.
Maps: OS Explorer OL 6 and 7, South-eastern area; Harvey Superwalker, Central Lakeland.
Refreshments: Old and New Dungeon Ghyll Hotels; The Wainwright Inn, Chapel Stile.
Public Transport: Langdale Rambler bus from Ambleside.

Left: *Magnificent Gimmer Crag.*

Below: *Harrison Stickle reflected in Blea Tarn.*

Leaving behind Pike o'Stickle's rocky summit the way ahead is north-west along a path across the open wastes of Martcrag Moor gradually descending to the small tarn at Stake Pass, crossed by an old packhorse route linking Langdale with Borrowdale via Langstrath. From the pass, a well-used path descends south-west into Langdale Combe, crossing Stake Gill before steep zigzags lead down below Black Crag. The path coming down Rossett Gill is joined at a wooden footbridge over Stake Gill.

The valley floor now widens and the Mickleden pastures are crossed along a wide path, eventually passing behind the Old Dungeon Ghyll Hotel. Continuing east the path passes below the popular climber's outcrop of Raven Crag back to Sticklebarn Tavern.

Striding Edge, the classic way up Helvellyn.

Opposite page, main picture: *Traversing the Dodds; Blencathra in the distance.*
Bottom left: *Ullswater from Gowbarrow Fell.*
Bottom right: *Approaching the summit of Fairfield.*

4   CENTRAL FELLS

The Dodds, the Helvellyn range and the Fairfield massif are three separate groups of hills which form a huge north-south barrier between the valleys of Thirlmere and Grasmere to the west, and Ullswater and Patterdale to the east. There is only one low point on this 25km/15.5 miles ridge, and with little re-ascent between the tops, it's the most continuous area of high-level fells in the district. Not surprisingly the ridge provides a magnificent and challenging walk.

Situated at the very heart of Lakeland these individual ranges provide some classic walks, including a circuit of the remote and grassy expanses of the Dodds, a traverse of Helvellyn's knife-edge ridges of Striding and Swirral Edges, and the ever-popular Fairfield Horseshoe above Wordsworth's Rydal. Seen from the west these central fells often appear rounded and smooth, but from the east they take on a much more rugged character, especially those overlooking Patterdale. Here a series of deep, crag-headed valleys cut into the fells creating some of the wildest and most spectacular scenery in the area, including Deepdale, Dovedale with its overhanging buttresses of Dove Crag, and Grisedale.

Situated 8km/5 miles north-west of Windermere, Ambleside is a popular, though very commercial base, for exploring these fells. Its narrow streets and cluster of grey-green stone houses are crowded with shops, several pubs and cafés. Ambleside has good bus links to centres such as Grasmere, Keswick and Windermere, including a summer service over the Kirkstone Pass to Patterdale and Glenridding, which are both excellent bases for several of the described walks. Ambleside offers a good range of accommodation, including a youth hostel, along with two others at nearby Grasmere. In the Patterdale area there are B&Bs, good camping sites at Brotherswater, Glenridding, and Patterdale and also youth hostels at Patterdale and Helvellyn.

Castle Rock of Triermain on the lower slopes of Watson's Dodd.

WALK 14 DOING THE DODDS

Starting from the small village of Dockray, with its collection of farms, cottages and a pub situated at the foot of Watermillock Common, this excellent circuit around the Dodds crosses the tops of Stybarrow Dodd, Watson's Dodd, Great Dodd and Clough Head, finally returning along the Old Coach Road from Keswick.

At first glance the smooth rolling grassy hills to the north of the Helvellyn range may have little to entice the keen fell walker. Unlike their neighbours there are no craggy combes or rocky ridges here. Even my old copy of Baddeley's guide to the Lake District describes a trip around the northern shoulder of the Dodds as 'one of the dullest walks in the district, the only redeeming feature being the views of Blencathra's ridges and the distant prospect of the Pennines beyond the Eden Valley' Don't be deceived though, for these massively sprawling hills – very reminiscent of the Howgills to the east – have a charm of their own and offer some of the easiest high-level walking in Lakeland.

Dockray to Stybarrow Dodd

Just south of the road bridge near the Royal Hotel in Dockray, a short lane leads to a gate giving access to the National Trust's Watermillock Common. A clear track is followed bearing left just before a ford then a path climbs to meet a boundary wall above Glencoyne Park. Here you have a superb view across Ullswater to the High Street fells on the eastern skyline. The path continues alongside the wall over the high ground on Brown Hills then along a grassy ridge to a wall crossing from where you can peer left down to the steep, rocky head of Glencoyne.

Heading up Matterdale Common to Great Dodd.

By taking a minor path right alongside the wall up steep slopes, you arrive at the memorial cairn at the top of Birkett Fell. This stretch of fell sloping to the east was given this name in 1963, in memory of Lord Birkett, a great advocate and lover of the Lake District. His greatest triumph was the role he played in preventing Ullswater being turned into a reservoir.

Just a gentle stroll to the west is Hart Side, whose grassy rounded summit with its cluster of cairns at 756m/2480 feet, overlooks Deep Dale to the north. To the south-west, beyond a dip in a broad ridge is Green Side, with its conspicuous cairns and scattered stones known as White Stones, visible on the skyline ahead. Green Side gives its name to the mines and road in Glenridding, where old spoil heaps still exist.

The steep road out of Dockray.

Aira Force.

Stybarrow Dodd, (843m/2766 feet), on the main ridge to Helvellyn, lies a short distance away to the west and is easily reached. From here you have tremendous views south to Raise, backed by Catstye Cam and Helvellyn, while to the west, across Thirlmere, a galaxy of peaks raise their heads as your eyes are drawn to the distant outlines of Great Gable and the Scafells. Apart from the views, the greatest attraction of the Dodds is that you can usually escape the crowds and wander for miles over gentle terrain.

However, it is in the depths of winter when there is a firm layer of consolidated snow underfoot, that these hills are at their best for both walkers and cross-country skiers alike. One of the finest ski-touring days I've ever experienced in the Lake District was a full circuit of the Dodds. The snow conditions and weather were perfect and our party of three didn't want the day to end. As it was, we cut it fine, and had to ski the last section wearing headlamps.

Aira Beck, which rises on the eastern slopes of Stybarrow Dodd, passes through Dockray, to eventually plunge down a ravine to form the spectacular waterfall of Aira Force, 5km /3 miles north of Glenridding. This 21m/70 feet high waterfall is spectacular when in spate and was the setting for Wordsworth's poem, *Somnambulist*. It's worth a visit when the tops are out of condition.

Approaching Great Dodd with Blencathra in the background.

Stybarrow Dodd to Dockray

The ridge now swings north-west to Watson's Dodd. Admitted it's all easy walking hereabouts with nothing very dramatic, but the area does have some special features. On the lower slopes of Watson's Dodd is the magnificent Castle Rock of Triermain, one of the finest crags in the area. The rocks were immortalised by Sir Walter Scott in his poem *The Bridal of Triermain.*

Veering north-east, the ridge leads towards the massive bulk of Great Dodd, the high point on a broad ridge overlooking Deepdale to the east and St John's Common to the west. Striding out you soon reach a large stone shelter and summit cairn of Great Dodd (857m/2811feet). This is a welcome oasis from where you get superb views and, with a little imagination, you can pick out most of Lakeland's high fells.

A superb winter's day on the Dodds.

The main ridge now descends south-west to Little Dodd then north-west to Calfhow Pike, with its fine vista down Matterdale to the right. Immediately north lies Clough Head, the last top on the circuit, which is easily approached up the open moor to its summit shelter and trig point at 726m/2381feet. The steep cliffs of the Red Screes, sitting below the northern edge of the flat grassy summit, make Clough Head one to the most attractive tops on the round, and the views are pretty good too. From here Blencathra dominates the skyline above Threlkeld, showing off its fine ridges and gullies, which look particularly alpine when plastered in snow.

Leaving Clough Head to the north-east, the rocky knoll of White Pike is passed on its right, before continuing down steep grassy slopes to join the Old Coach Road linking Dockray with Wanthwaite in St John's in the Vale. Once used by horse-drawn vehicles, the rough track is now popular with mountain bikers. Turning right here the track leads across Mariel Bridge, passing below Wolf Crags situated on the right, and eventually emerging through a gate onto a road at a T-junction. The narrow road straight ahead descends steeply east for about a 1.6km/1 mile back to Dockray.

INFORMATION
Start/Finish: Parking near Dockray road bridge by the Royal Hotel, GR: 393216.
Distance: 18km/11.2 miles.
Walking Time/total climb: 6-8 hours/900m (2952 feet).
Grading: Difficult; a high level walk on good paths over rolling fells. In poor visibility, good navigational skills are needed on the featureless tops.
Maps: OS Explorer OL 5, the English Lakes – North Eastern area; Harvey Superwalker, Lakeland Central.
Refreshments: Royal Hotel, Dockray and Traveller's Rest, Glenridding.
Public Transport: Train to Penrith and bus service to Glenridding.

Swirral Edge and Catstye Cam.

WALK 15 CATSTYE CAM AND SWIRRAL EDGE

The pyramidal-shaped hill of Catstye Cam (or Catstycam) to the west of Glenridding in Patterdale, dominates this walk around the rims of Brown and Kepple Coves. Catstye Cam, its old name being Catechedam, is a lovely isolated peak linked by Swirral Edge to Helvellyn and, despite the popularity of its neighbour, is rarely crowded. There are excellent views along the walk, especially from the tops of Helvellyn and Catstye Cam. Relics of a bygone age when lead mining was an important industry are also explored along the way.

Glenridding to Catstye Cam

Glenridding, a small village consisting of little more than a couple of rows of cottages, lies at the southern end of Ullswater, and is now the busiest of the lake's settlements. Formerly a tiny hamlet, it grew in importance with the development of the Greenside Lead Mine.

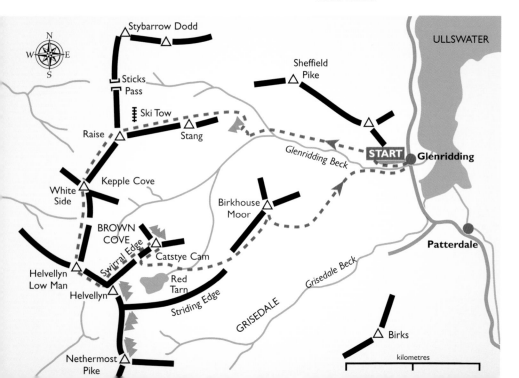

From Glenridding, the Greenside Road climbs west above the village, passing a row of former miners' cottages above Glenridding Beck. Here the road degenerates as it continues past Glenridding Youth Hostel, one of the old mine buildings, overlooked by Greenside's abandoned mines. The mines were worked on a small scale from about 1775, reaching a peak in the early nineteenth century. Red Tarn, on the slopes of Helvellyn, and tarns in Brown and Kepple Coves supplied water for the mine and the remains of leats and sluices can be found on the surrounding fells.

106

Catstye Cam across Kepple Cove.

The path leading to Helvellyn Lower Man.

At the top of the road, by an outdoor pursuits centre, a sign for Sticks Pass points the way up a track to the right which eventually zigzags its way steeply below Stang End's broken crags. When a broad, grassy col is reached, it's just an amble along the path towards some spoil tips, before heading left towards an obvious stone ditch known as The Chimney. This long channel, terminating at a short stack, is the remnant of a long flue, now collapsed, which fed air to the hearths at the lead smelting mill down the hillside at the foot of Lucy Tongue Gill. Prior to this, lead ore was transported by packhorse trains, initially over Sticks Pass to the smelting works at Derwent Water and later to Alston Moor.

After a steep climb the path flattens out near the old chimney base – now a useful windbreak – beyond which a faint path up steep grassy slopes lead up to the rocky summit of Raise (883m/2897 feet). The pylons visible on your right are part of England's highest ski tow. This modern button ski tow is owned by the Lake District Ski Club and despite recent mild winters, the northern flanks of Raise retain snow for longer than most slopes in the area, and you may find some good skiing here most years. The hills surrounding Raise, especially the Dodds to the north, are also excellent ski-touring terrain.

Looking back from Lower Man to White Side.

Catstye Cam and Helvellyn from Raise.

From the summit of Raise you have a wonderful panoramic view of peaks, especially the smooth, rounded tops of the Dodds rolling to the north beyond Sticks Pass, with the full length of Ullswater to the right. Down to the left is Kepple Cove whose tarn was breached during a storm in 1927, the ensuing flood causing a great deal of damage in the valley below.

A wide, cairned path now leads south along a broad ridge, skirting the rim of Kepple Cove before rising steadily up to the top of White Side (863m/2831 feet). Here you can look north across the Vale of Keswick to Skiddaw, while to the east is the rugged Brown Cove backed by the dominant Catstye Cam with the graceful sweep of Swirral Edge linking it to Helvellyn clearly visible.

Descending Swirral Edge towards Catsye Cam.

Topping out onto Helvellyn's summit plateau.

Catstye Cam's easy south-west ridge.

A frozen Red Tarn below Helvellyn.

Ahead, the stony path eventually follows the crest of a narrowing ridge over the stony top of Helvellyn Lower Man (925m/3034 feet) before swinging up left to the Helvellyn plateau. The rim of Brown Cove leads easily round to the top of Swirral Edge where you can take in one of the great views of Lakeland; that of Red Tarn in a hollow below Helvellyn's rocky east face and enclosed by the encircling arms of Striding and Swirral Edges. However, it is the wedge-shaped Catstye Cam, the next peak on the circuit, which will get most attention. Having got this close it would be a pity not to take the edge path round to the nearby summit of Helvellyn.

Back at the top of Swirral Edge, broken rocks lead steeply down a narrow ridge to a path which weaves its way along the steep ridge, sometimes on the crest and at other times down rocky slopes on the right-hand side. Although it is fairly exposed, the difficulties are not too great, but care is needed in windy conditions. When plastered in snow the descent is much more serious and axe and crampons are often needed. Also large cornices, prone to collapse, often build up here in the lee of the wind and care is needed under such conditions. The gradient eventually eases to a col at the

Walkers at the top of Swirral Edge.

Sunset from Helvellyn with Skiddaw in the distance.

foot of Catstye Cam's south-west ridge which is easily ascended up to the isolated summit of Catstye Cam (890m/2919 feet).

From Catstye Cam's top you can peer down Ullswater, with the High Street range filling the skyline to the east. However, the finest vista is of the craggy east face of Helvellyn sweeping up above Red Tarn, with the dragon's-back profile of Striding Edge beyond, usually with groups of walkers silhouetted against the sky on its crest.

Catstye Cam to Glenridding

After admiring the views, Catstye Cam's east ridge can be descended along a faint path, vague in places, over steep scree and grass and, when convenient, you could contour right to join the broad track near the Red Tarn outlet. However, it's much easier to retrace your steps back down to the dip where a wide path leads more gently down to Red Tarn.

Sheltered from the prevailing westerlies by the bulky summit plateau, the east face of Helvellyn above Red Tarn is exposed to any Arctic blizzards sweeping in from the north-east. Then, the scalloped hillside with its snow-plastered buttresses and gullies, becomes a winter playground for mountaineers.

Once across Red Tarn beck, a broad track leads east up to the 'Hole-in-the-Wall' on the skyline ahead. Here a fainter path swings left alongside the wall on a boggy ridge towards the summit of Birkhouse Moor. The constructed path eventually veers east and descends the steep right bank of Mires Beck to the campsite by Glenridding Beck. Here you turn right and take a riverside track alongside the campsite to join a lane leading back into Glenridding.

INFORMATION
Start/Finish: Glenridding, GR: 386169.
Distance: 14km/8.7 miles.
Walking Time/total climb: 6 hours/981m (3219 feet).
Grading: Difficult; a high mountain route mainly on good paths and with a steep, exposed descent of Swirral Edge.
Maps: OS Explorer OL 5; Harvey Superwalker, Lakeland Central.
Refreshments: The Traveller's Rest, Glenridding.
Public Transport: Rail service to Penrith with buses to Patterdale and Glenridding.

Catstye Cam catches the last light of a winter's day.

Walkers leaving Grisedale for Helvellyn.

WALK 16 HELVELLYN AND THE GRISEDALE HORSESHOE

Starting from the picturesque village of Patterdale on the south-western corner of Ullswater, this superb high level walk follows the skyline rim around Grisedale (a Norse name meaning the valley of the pigs), which cuts deeply into the eastern flanks of the Helvellyn massif. The walk crosses St Sunday Crag, Dollywaggon and Nethermost Pikes, finally returning along Helvellyn's airy Striding Edge to Grisedale. Throughout the circuit you have superb views into hidden combes, valleys, and across lakes and fells stretching to distant horizons.

Grisedale Bridge to Helvellyn

From Grisedale Bridge, on the A592 about mid-way between Patterdale and Grisedale, a minor road runs a short way up into Grisedale on the south side of the beck. Near the top of the hill road a footpath leads off left across a field, then weaves its way steeply through scattered crags to Thornhow End. From here you can look across to Ullswater in an exquisite setting, nestling below rolling fells.

Below right: *Ullswater backed by the Helvellyn range.*

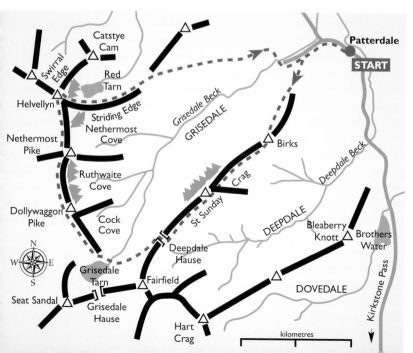

Dollywaggon Pike from St Sunday Crag.

The Helvellyn range from St Sunday Crag.

Airy scrambling on Pinnacle Ridge, St Sunday Crag.

The path rises across the fell to reach the grassy crest of a ridge climbing steadily up to the top of Birks (622m/2041 feet). Continuing across undulating terrain it's a steady walk with a final steep pull up the ridge to the summit rocks of St Sunday Crag, where a huge cairn sits just north of its highest point at 841m/2759 feet. There is a tremendous feeling of space here, with the green valley of Deepdale on the left and Grisedale to the right, backed by Nethermost Cove and crowned by Striding Edge. Ahead the broken buttresses of Cofa Pike and Fairfield look very impressive.

Situated on St Sunday Crag's north-western flank is one of the finest ridge scrambles in Lakeland, namely Pinnacle Ridge, a 182m/600 feet classic Grade 3 scramble. The highlight of the scramble is an exposed crossing of a series of sharp pinnacles at the top of the ridge, which ends just below the summit slopes of St Sunday Crag. For experienced scramblers an ascent of Pinnacle Ridge combined with a crossing of Striding Edge is a mountain day *par excellence*.

Crossing St Sunday Crag.

St Sunday Crag from Deepdale Hause.

Grisedale Tarn from Dollywaggon Pike.

Leading gently south-west from the top of St Sunday Crag, a narrowing ridge drops to the dip at Deepdale Hause where the main path forks. Here you branch right along a path, which traverses across grassy slopes down to Grisedale Tarn, the lowest point on the Helvellyn range. Grisedale Tarn is famous for being the parting of the ways of William Wordsworth and his brother John, who was later drowned at sea. The event is commemorated by a plaque just north of the tarn at Brothers Rock. The sheltered, grassy banks of the tarn provide a good resting place from where you can contemplate having to regain all that lost height.

A wide, eroded footpath zigzags steeply up the hillside above Grisedale Tarn to Dollywaggon Pike. After the steep plod it's a delight to walk along the path across the broad ridge which rolls gently over Dollywaggon Pike (858m/2815 feet) and Nethermost Pike (891m/2923 feet). To visit both summits it's worth leaving the main path at the first opportunity and contouring around the rim of the plateau overlooking the craggy depths of Ruthwaite Cove and Nethermost Cove. All along this section you can look back across Grisedale to St Sunday Crag, but most likely your eyes will be drawn across to the chiseled arête of Striding Edge, one of the most popular easy scrambles in the Lake District.

The broad path climbs steadily onto Helvellyn's summit plateau with its four-bay wall shelter and huge pile of stones, which marks the top (950m/3117feet). Although Helvellyn's flat top is rather a dull place, it makes up for it by its magnificent panoramic views, which embrace most of Lakeland. The summit is a great vantage point especially east to the High Street range. I never cease to be amazed by the fact that a light aircraft landed on the plateau in 1926, an event recorded by a passenger who was a staff photographer for the *Manchester Evening News*.

Helvellyn to Grisedale

Helvellyn is one of the most visited high tops in Lakeland, so expect the summit area to be busy. However, by leaving a crossing of Striding Edge until late in the day you might have the place to yourself. At the south-eastern corner of the summit plateau, on the brink of the descent to Striding Edge, is the Gough Memorial. Charles Gough died in 1805 after falling in this area, an event immortalized by Sir Walter Scott and also by Wordsworth, mainly because Gough's faithful terrier remained with the body until discovered three months later.

The hard way up Helvellyn.

The final scramble to Helvellyn's top.

Striding Edge and Red Tarn.

Above: *A winter crossing of Striding Edge.*

Right: *Heading around Nethermost Cove to Helvellyn.*

INFORMATION

Start/Finish: Grisedale Bridge, GR: 390161. Car parking in Patterdale and Glenridding

Distance: 17km/10.6 miles.

Walking Time/total climb: 6 hours/1341m (4400 feet).

Grading: Very Difficult; a high-level mountain traverse across steep terrain with some easy scrambling. Can be serious under winter conditions.

Maps: OS Explorer OL5; Harvey Superwalker, Lakeland Central.

Refreshments: The White Lion at Patterdale and The Traveller's Rest at Glenridding.

Public Transport: Rail service to Penrith with buses to Patterdale and Glenridding.

Beyond the memorial it's a steep descent over polished rocks and paths covered in scree to a rocky gap. Beyond the gap, a short scramble on large holds up a shallow polished groove lands you onto Striding Edge proper. This awkward stretch can be bypassed along a path descending on the right-hand side of the rocks, regaining the ridge further along.

The crest of the ridge is good rock and quite narrow in places, though not too difficult. Crossing over some of the minor rocky pinnacles creates a great sense of height and exposure with very steep slopes sweeping down either side. The traverse is a sheer delight, but on windy days the eroded paths just below the knife-edge crest are a much safer alternative. In winter when the rocks are covered in snow and ice, Striding Edge is the domain of experienced mountaineers. Then a crossing of Striding and Swirral Edges is one of the best winter excursions in Lakeland.

Striding Edge and Helvellyn.

The main path from Red Tarn.

Down to the left below the steep rocky east face of Helvellyn, is Red Tarn set in a glacier-carved hollow between Swirral and Striding Edges and backed by the wedge-shaped peak of Catstye Cam.

Beyond High Spying How, the rocky tooth that marks the end of Striding Edge, a broad stony path descends to the 'Hole in the Wall'. From here you take the wide path slanting east down the fell side, eventually dropping right to cross Grisedale Beck to meet the hill road leading back to Grisedale Bridge.

117

Deepdale from Fairfield's summit.

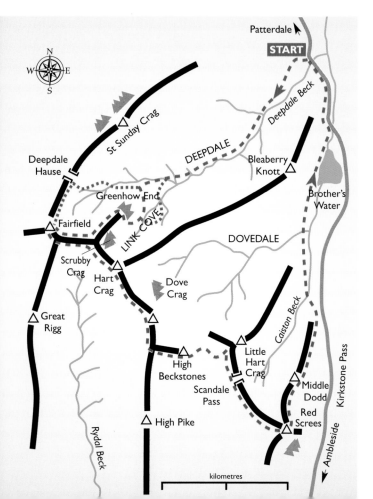

WALK 17 FAIRFIELD FROM THE EAST

Fairfield (the light coloured peak) is the high point of a group of fells overlooking Ambleside to the south, and is often climbed from that direction via the ever-popular Fairfield Horseshoe, which curves around the deep valley of Rydale.

However, an alterative and more rugged approach is from the east via Deepdale, and is arguably the finest way up Fairfield. Deepdale only reveals its secrets to those prepared to explore its upper reaches where Fairfield's summit hides behind vast, fortress-like rocky buttresses. At the head of the valley, Link Cove and the broad ridge above Greenhow End provide a fine way up to Fairfield's retiring summit plateau. There is also the option of some superb scrambling up Link Cove Gill and Greenhow End. From Fairfield the return leg takes in the wide ridge over Hart Crag, Dove Crag and Red Screes before finally descending to Brother's Water.

Patterdale to Fairfield

Starting at Bridgend on the A592 road just south of the village of Patterdale, a rough track leads past Deepdale Hall, eventually narrowing to a footpath which continues into the valley. On the right are the bulky heights of St Sunday Crag, with the long rugged skyline of Hartsop above How to your left. Deeper into the valley, the rocky prow of Greenhow End at the end of the spur from Fairfield, dominates the view. Greenhow End splits the valley head into two coves, Link Cove on the left and Sleet Cove to the right.

The main path crosses an area of drumlins – humps left behind by glacial action – before ascending across steep slopes on the right-hand flank of Sleet Cove. The path eventually reaches Deepdale Hause, the dip between St Sunday Crag and Fairfield. By turning left here, the steep rocky ridge over Cofa Pike leads up to Fairfield's summit.

A more challenging way is via Link Cove which is reached from the main Deepdale path along a fainter one sneaking off left in front of Mart Crag. Grassy slopes on the left-hand side of Greenhow End lead into Link Cove. This is an exquisite, rugged place with Scrubby Crag forming its impressive head wall and looking more like a hanging Scottish corrie than a Lakeland cove.

For competent scramblers, the cove can also be reached by following the tree-lined Link Cove Gill further to the left. This is one of the most entertaining gill scrambles (Grade 3) in Lakeland, and is best climbed during a spell of dry weather. In spate conditions, the easy slabs on the right of the gill can be followed. When the ravine eventually merges into the hillside, you simply head up right across grassy slopes into Link Cove.

From Link Cove an obvious ascending line of weakness can be easily picked out up to the left of the crags of Greenhow End before easier ground leads back right up grass and scree to a grassy ridge with Scrubby Crag well to the left. Scramblers who followed Link Cove Gill might wish to tackle the light coloured slabs on the left flank of Greenhow End. These provide enjoyable and continuous Grade 1 scrambling up clean rocky ribs, interspersed with slabs and rocky steps, which lead pleasantly to the top of Greenhow End. Here you can pause and enjoy the view down the trench of Deepdale with the High Street fells as a backcloth.

Scrambling up Greenhow End.

The craggy head of Deepdale.

Above Greenhow End.

The Greenhow End ridge leading to Fairfield.

It's now just a gentle walk up the grass and rocky ridge to meet a wide path leading right to Fairfield's summit at 873m/2864 feet. As height is gained memorable views unfold, particularly across Sleet Cove to the rocky summit of Cofa Pike backed by the craggy eastern coves of the Helvellyn range. Fairfield's top is the hub of many popular walks and is often crowded, especially on summer weekends. However, in misty conditions this complex plateau with steep drops to the north can be a trap for the unwary and great care is needed.

Fairfield to Bridgend

The return leg starts along the eastern section of the classic Fairfield Horseshoe circuit. A cairned path contours east around the head of Link Cove accompanied by fine views south down the long valley of Rydal Beck to Ambleside and beyond to Windermere. You soon arrive at Hart Crag (822m/2696 feet), from where there is a good escape route east along Hartsop above How, the long ridge separating Dovedale from Deepdale.

After descending the long, stony crest of Hart Crag south-east to a dip, a grassy ascent alongside a wall leads up to the top of Dove Crag (792m/2598 feet), from where you can peer east down to Brother's Water. Continuing south alongside the wall to a large cairn, a narrow path branches off left to a set of cairns at High Bakestones. Sadly, many of the previously tall cairns have been vandalized.

Leaving the cairns, a steep path drops east down the fellside to the broad marshy depression of Bakestones Moss, then bears left up to the cairned rocky top of the first and highest summit of Little Hart Crag at 637m/2090 feet. From here you can look into Dovedale to the north and Scandale to the south. Heading south from between the twin tops, the path veers past Scandale Tarn then down to the crest of Scandale Pass, once the line of a packhorse route linking Glenridding with Ambleside. Another escape route leads off left here down Caiston Glen to Brother's Water.

Beyond the pass the path continues alongside the wall for the final ascent of the day up to a trig point, cairn and wind shelter at the top of Red Screes (776m/2545 feet),

just beyond a small tarn. From the cairn high above Raven Crag, you have a bird's-eye-view of Kirkstone Pass and its summit inn, at 457m/1500 feet, the highest pub in the Lake District. The summit also offers superb views particularly north down Patterdale to Ullswater.

It's all downhill now; and very steep. A path follows the crest of Red Scree's north ridge over Middle Dodd, before plunging to its base where a small footbridge crosses Caiston Beck. Beyond the footbridge the path continues around the base of High Hartsop Dodd, past the imposing Hartsop Hall and along the wooded shore of Brother's Water to Cow Bridge. From here the road, combined with a low-level footpath through woodland, leads to Bridgend.

Above left: Approaching Fairfield from Cofa Pike and St Sunday Crag.

Above right: Crossing Fairfield backed by the Helvellyn range.

INFORMATION

Start/Finish: Lay-by at Bridgend on the A592 road 1.5km/I mile south of Patterdale, GR: 399143

Distance: 18km/11.2 miles

Walking Time/total climb: 6-8 hours/1080m (3543 feet).

Grading: Very Difficult; a high mountain walk along mainly good footpaths but with some steep terrain at the head of Deepdale. Best avoided in misty weather. There is an option to include some scrambling.

Maps: OS Explorer OL 5; Harvey Superwalker, Lakeland Central.

Refreshments: Brotherswater Inn and the White Lion Inn, Patterdale.

Public Transport: Rail service to Penrith with buses to Patterdale and Glenridding.

Red Screes overlooking Honister Pass.

Exploring the Martindale Fells.

Storm on the Longsleddale skyline.

5   EASTERN FELLS

Between the A592 Ullswater to Windermere and the A6 Kendal to Penrith via Shap is a vast area of rolling hills known as the Eastern Fells. The western side of this complex group is typical Lakeland terrain, rugged and craggy, while on the eastern side the hills are more rounded and cloaked in grass and heather, much more akin to the neighbouring Pennines.

The main spine of the Eastern Fells is the long ridge of the High Street range, whose main claim to fame is its Roman Road, which stretches for more than 30km/18.5 miles from Penrith to Ambleside and rises to over 600m/1968 feet above sea level. It is one of the Romans' most spectacular highways, which now provides a superb long walk starting from Pooley Bridge, on the northern shore of Ullswater, and finishing at Ambleside. Being the highest, the High Street range is the most popular of these fells and provides some excellent shorter walks from Hartsop, near Patterdale, and Mardale on the eastern side at the head of Haweswater Reservoir.

The gentler fells, particularly on the south-eastern flanks, contain a series of isolated valleys including Longsleddale, Bannisdale and the Kent valley, whose skylines offer challenging horseshoe walks, the best of these being around Kentmere and Longsleddale. When the weather is poor there are also plenty of low-level walks around Place Fell and the Martindale fells near Pooley Bridge. There are also walks along the eastern shore of Ullswater, with the option of returning via lake steamer.

The area can be explored from Ambleside, Kendal, Windermere and the Ullswater/Patterdale area. There are campsites at Kendal, Patterdale, Brother's Water, and Pooley Bridge, with youth hostels at Patterdale, Ambleside, Windermere and Kendal. There are bus services from Penrith to Patterdale, and between Kendal, Windermere and Ambleside.

Blea Water from High Street.

Below left: High Street from the Straits of Riggindale.

Below right: Froswick on the Kentmere Horseshoe.

The summit of High Street.

Below right: *Ullswater and the High Street fells.*

WALK 18 HIGH STREET BARGAINS

There are several popular ways up High Street but my personal favourite, and a very quiet ascent, starts from Hartsop and follows an undulating, switchback circuit. The walk involves an ascent of the broad ridge overlooking the village to Stoney Cove Pike then climbs up to Thornthwaite Crag. After crossing High Street, the return is via Rest Dodd, Angletarn Pikes and Boredale Hause. It's a gem of a route.

Seen from a distance, especially from the west, the High Street range looks particularly smooth and you can see why the Romans were attracted to it. Of all the roads built by the Romans in Britain the one across High Street, connecting the forts of *Brocavum*, near Penrith, and *Gala*, on the shores of Windermere, is certainly the most impressive and audacious.

Also, according to Mrs E Lynn Lynton writing in a *Lakes Country* publication of 1854, High Street is 'More like a common than a mountain.' But don't be put off by this description, for on closer inspection you will find High Street doesn't show off its finest features; you have to seek those out. And there are certainly plenty to find; unspoilt valleys such as Riggindale, Randale, Rampsgill and Cauldale, along with rocky ridges and rugged, crag-girted combes biting into the flanks of High Street are what give it its character.

The Helvellyn range from Hartsop Dodd.

Threshthwaite Mouth and Cauldale Moor.

Hartsop to High Street

The day begins at the ancient village of Hartsop, just off the A592 road opposite Brother's Water near the foot of the Kirkstone Pass. This beautiful village, with its houses of blue slate and seventeenth century spinning galleries overlooked by the steep slopes of Hartsop Dodd, is very popular with tourists and walkers alike. So get there early.

Just beyond the car park at the end of the village, a footbridge crosses Hayeswater Gill, from where a path rises steeply alongside a wall up to the open fellside. Eventually a broad grassy ridge is joined leading left up to Hartsop Dodd. As height is gained, you have fine views down to Hartsop backed by Ullswater. The path continues alongside a wall climbing steadily for nearly 2km/1.25 miles up to the desolate summit plateau of Stoney Cove Pike (763m/2503 feet) whose lower top has the unusual name of John Bell's Banner. The word 'banner' means boundary, and the top is thought to be named after the Rev. John Bell whose parish boundary stretched this far from Ambleside in the sixteenth century.

The southern prospect from Thornthwaite Crag.

Secluded Hayeswater.

Stoney Cove Pike is a complex peak with several ridges and on its northern flanks is the fine cirque of Thornthwaite Cove overlooking the beautiful valley of Pasture Beck – another lovely approach route. To the west, across Kirkstone Pass, is the bulky Red Screes and to its right the Helvellyn-Fairfield range fills the skyline. The trio of shapely conical peaks to the south-west is Yoke, Ill Bell and Froswick, which rise between Troutbeck and Kentmere.

From a staggered wall junction near the top of Stoney Cove Pike, a path descends steeply into the rocky gap of Threshthwaite Mouth, followed by an equally steep climb up the other side to Thornthwaite Crag, complete with its spectacular drystone chimney-like cairn set in a wall above outcropping rocks. Since Victorian times this top has been renowned as a great viewpoint and on clear days you can have great fun trying to identify the complex jumble of hills to the west. The top is also the turning point for walkers doing the Kentmere Round, and visible to the south is the long ridge leading up to the rocky top of Froswick.

Magnificent snow conditions on High Street.

Heading across the Straits of Riggindale to High Street.

Refreshment break at the top of High Street.

High Street and the Roman Road.

The well-marked rutted course of the Roman Road, rising left, can be followed across the western slopes of High Street. If you want to reach the actual top of High Street – and who wouldn't? – then you need to branch right along a path beside a wall which crosses grassy, almost rock-free terrain leading up to the summit trig point at 828m/2718 feet. There are great views west to the scalloped combes of Fairfield and Helvellyn, while from the eastern edge of the summit plateau you get an imposing view into the depths of Blea Water, in a hollow at the foot of the steep, verdant rocky slopes.

On the OS map, the summit of High Street is shown as Racecourse Hill, a reminder of the days when local villagers held horse races and various sporting events, including wrestling, on this broad, grassy arena. For many competitors, greater emphasis was probably placed on revelry and merriment rather than athletic endeavor. The last annual fair was held in 1835. During a good snow cover, High Street's smooth summit slopes provides excellent cross-country skiing.

High Street to Hartsop

Leaving the summit, the path continues north alongside the wall around the grassy rim of the plateau and leads gently down to the Straits of Riggindale, where the track of the Roman Road is rejoined. The track climbs a little before swinging round the subsidiary summit of The Knott. The walk can be shortened from here by heading left down a steep path to Hayeswater and then following a rough track beside Hayeswater Gill to Hartsop.

The main walk continues north alongside the wall, which leads nearly up to the top of Rest Dodd. From the summit cairn at 696m/2283 feet you can enjoy the splendid view over Martindale. If time permits, then a slight detour up right to the top of Kidsty Pike is highly recommended for a stunning view east down into the remote valley of Riggindale, where golden eagles nest and wild ponies roam the hillsides.

Descending west from Rest Dodd a path is joined which threads a way through the rocky and hummocky terrain of Satura Crags before dropping down to the lapping

The northern view from High Street to The Knott.

Rest Dodd and The Nab viewed from The Knott.

waters of the unusually-shaped Angle Tarn. The path climbs beyond the tarn and winds its way round Angletarn Pikes, from where you can look back up the Ullswater Valley to Hartsop Dodd and Brother's Water, backed by Red Screes and Fairfield. The narrow path crosses the steep fellside north down to the dip at Boredale Hause, a major junction where several paths meet at the foot of Place Fell's south ridge.

Here you swing sharp left and follow a path across the steep hillside down to the valley bottom through which Goldrill Beck gently flows. A good path and track now lead south below pleasant wooded and bracken-covered slopes to the join the narrow road on the edge of Hartsop.

Approaching the top of Long Stile backed by Haweswater.

WALK 19 AROUND MARDALE HEAD

This excellent outing explores the rugged skyline around Mardale Head overlooking the southern end of Haweswater, and approaches High Street via the classic ridge of Rough Crag and Long Stile; a personal favourite. The walk continues over Mardale Ill Bell and Harter Fell before crossing the gentler grassy hills of Branstree and Selside Pike, returning via the Corpse Road and Haweswater's shoreline.

From the top of High Street, with its east-facing, ice-carved coves and crag-girted tarns, you can peer down into the valley containing the Haweswater Reservoir. The valley hasn't always looked like this though. Originally it was populated by the farming villages of Measand and Mardale Green and contained the two small natural lakes of High Water and Low Water. But that all changed in 1935 when the valley was flooded to create the controversial Haweswater Reservoir to provide water for Manchester. The water level rose by 29m/95 feet to create a single lake 6.5km/4 miles long. At the time, the construction of the dam wall was revolutionary, and consists of a unique hollow-buttress structure – the first in the world – with 44 separate buttresses linked by flexible joints.

Mardale Head to High Street

From the car park at Mardale Head a path leads across the flat dale, crossing Mardale Beck then swings right to follow the shore of Haweswater Reservoir. Before reaching the forest at the end of The Rigg – the finger of land protruding into Haweswater – another path branches up left to the crest of a ridge. Turning left here a wall is followed along the ridge up Rough Crag towards High Street.

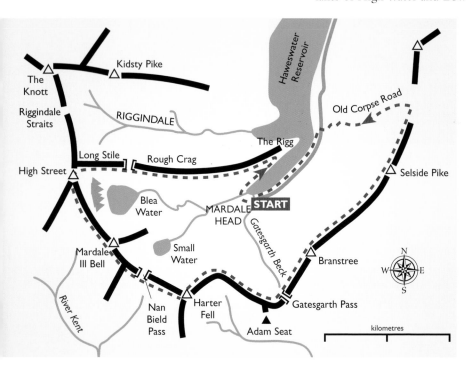

High Street and Haweswater from the Old Corpse Road.

As height is gained you can peer right into the remote valley of Riggindale. If you are very lucky you might even see a golden eagle here. There has been an eyrie here since the 1970s and Riggindale is now an RSPB reserve. It is a reflection of the wildness of these eastern valleys that eagles nest here – the only place in England. Down to the left is an imposing view to Blea Water, with a depth of 64m/210 feet, the deepest tarn in the Lake District.

The ridge eventually descends to the saddle of Caspel Gate with its small tarn, separating High Street from Rough Crag. Beyond Rough Crag the final section looks quite intimidating up the rocky spur of Long Stile but there are no real obstacles and the final delight is to suddenly emerge onto the summit plateau. The change in terrain is quite dramatic as you leave behind the exposed ridge and stroll across grass to a wall and the nearby trig point at 828m/2718 feet. From High Street's summit you get a great view west to the Fairfield and Helvellyn ranges.

A winter crossing of High Street.

The Nan Bield Pass and Harter Fell.

Harter Fell's summit.

INFORMATION

Start/Finish: Mardale Head car park, GR: 469107.

Distance: 17km/10.5 miles.

Walking Time/total climb: 6 hours/1500m (4920 feet).

Grading: Very Difficult; a rugged fell walk on mainly clear paths with some steep ascents and descents.

Maps: OS Explorer OL 5; Harvey Superwalker, Lakeland East.

Refreshments: The Walkers' Bar, Haweswater Hotel and the Mardale Inn, Bampton.

Public Transport: Limited summer bus service from Penrith.

High Street to Mardale Head

The eastern leg of the walk starts with a traverse to Mardale Ill Bell round the rim of the rugged cliffs sweeping up from Blea Water. From Ill Bell's stony summit, in a commanding position above Mardale, a stony track drops south through a wilderness of shattered rocks to the walled shelter at Nan Bield Pass, a good escape route in bad weather via Small Water. This narrow pass, slung between narrow rocky ridges linking Mardale Ill Bell with Harter Fell, is the high point on the old packhorse route between Mardale and Kentmere. During the descent to the pass you can look left down to Small Water, backed by Haweswater. On a clear day Morecambe Bay and the Irish Sea can be seen to the south-west.

An equally steep ascent now leads up to Harter Fell, its summit cairn at 778m/2552 feet adorned with iron posts. This is a good place to stop for refreshments and soak up the impressive views across to High Street before contouring east around the edge of the summit plateau to Little Harter Fell. From here another steep path descends to Gatesgarth Pass, an old packhorse route linking Mardale with Longsleddale. Beyond the pass a path is followed north-east up grassy slopes to the broad summit of Branstree, a circular basin trig point and little cairn marking its high point at 713m/2339 feet.

The next objective is Selside Pike, its top visible along a broad, undulating grassy ridge to the north-east. Easy walking along a path on the western side of a fence leads to the rocky shoulder of Artlecrag Pike, its top adorned with two tall cairns. From this airy perch you have superb views of High Street and Haweswater.

Just down the slopes off to the right, and worth a slight detour, is a conspicuous stone-built tall survey column, erected by engineers during construction of the Longsleddale aqueduct. There are several of these columns on the surrounding hills and they were used as line-of-sight measuring points for surveying the course of the tunnel beneath the fells to carry water from Haweswater to Manchester

Back at the path a broad grassy saddle is crossed from where it's just a gentle stroll up to the large shelter cairn at Selside Pike (655m/2149 feet). Apart from the High

Above: *Haweswater from Harter Fell.*

Left: *High Street from Harter Fell.*

Street range you can also appreciate the view north down Swindale to the Pennines, while to the east are the less visited Shap Fells rising beyond the trench of Mosedale. Continuing north, the grassy path gradually descends over the shoulder of Selside End to the high point of the Old Corpse Road. This is the route along which coffins were carried from Mardale via Swindale for burial in the churchyard in the village of Shap, before the graveyard at Mardale was consecrated in 1729. When the valley was flooded the exhumed bodies from the churchyard at Mardale were re-interred at Shap.

The Corpse Road, mainly a wide grassy path, now leads pleasantly left towards Haweswater. At the top of a series of steep zig zags just above the reservoir, are several ruined barns, which act as a foreground for superb views across Haweswater to The Rig backed by the High Street skyline crossed earlier. Once the valley road is reached a shoreline path leads back to the car park.

Crossing Artlecrag Pike backed by Selside Pike.

The upper reaches of Longsleddale.

WALK 20 A LONGSLEDDALE LOOP

Longsleddale, along with the isolated valleys of Mosedale, Swindale, Borrowdale and Bannisdale, cut into the flanks of the breezy fells across Eastern Lakeland. These are lonely places where you can walk for miles around valley rims through a landscape more akin to the Pennines than the Lakeland fells.

This outing follows the skyline around the head of Longsleddale and includes ascents of Grey Crag, Tarn Crag, Branstree, Harter Fell and Kentmere Pike, all of which offer fine views. Although the surrounding hills are not that high, what they lack in height they make up with their splendid isolation, far away from the crowds.

Entering the long, straight valley from the A6, just north of Kendal, you drive through an area of lush green fields, whitewashed farms and cottages strung out along the valley sides which are dotted with deciduous woods. The road through the dale, which has a pleasant, uncommercial and tranquil feel about it, ends at Sadgill Farm, the last farm up the valley. The farm overlooks a lovely packhorse bridge under which the aptly-named River Sprint dashes after its tumultuous journey down rocky staircases, narrow gorges and rocky pools from its source high in Wren Gill, beneath Harter Fell.

There is a car park at the road head, beyond which a rough track leads up to the wild and craggy head of the valley. This transition from gentle pastureland to the rugged valley head is brought about by the geological change from soft Silurian slates to the hard Borrowdale volcanic rocks, which form the craggy profiles of Goat Scar and Buckbarrow Crag visible ahead, either side of the track.

The view west across Longsleddale from Great Howe.

Sadgill to Branstree

From the car park a gate leads to a waymarked path, which ascends grassy and rocky slopes up the open fellside on the lower south-western flanks of Great Howe. As part of an ongoing preservation plan to protect the future of mountain juniper trees in the Lake District, threatened by overgrazing from sheep, some trees have been planted in inaccessible areas on the crags below Great Howe. Once you reach the top of Great Howe, you are rewarded by superb views up the valley and across to Kentmere Pike.

Beyond Great Howe the path heads north-east up grassy terrain to the small summit cairn on Grey Crag (638m/2093 feet). Setting off north from here you cross some

Kentmere Pike from Great Howe.

Raven Crag and Kentmere Pike from Tarn Crag.

rough, boggy terrain and peat hags to the slightly lower summit of Tarn Crag at 664m/2178 feet. The actual summit, which is rather boggy and surrounded by small rocky outcrops, is made all the more conspicuous by the nearby chimney-like stone and concrete survey column. The column was used during the construction of the Longsleddale aqueduct for carrying water from Haweswater Reservoir to Manchester.

The views from here across Longsleddale to the craggy eastern slopes of Kentmere Pike are particularly fine while the rolling moors to the east are very reminiscent of the Pennines and 'bog-trotters' will feel quite at home here, especially in misty weather with few landmarks to aid navigation. Don't underestimate these seductive, gentle hills though, for in poor visibility, sloppy compass work will be punished. Although once you find the main fence, which crosses much of the high ground, it can be a welcome waymarker when the 'clag' descends.

The fence line leads gently down to a broad, marshy col at the head of Mosedale, a desolate and remote valley cutting through the Shap Fells. You might even be lucky here and catch a glimpse of the elusive deer which roam these fells, sharing the grassy slopes with sheep. Straight ahead is Selside Brow up which a path climbs to the broad summit of Branstree (713m/2339 feet) with little going for it except the vista across to High Street.

Branstree to Sadgill

By following the fence south-east down steep grassy slopes Gatesgarth Pass, an old packhorse route linking Mardale with Longsleddale, is reached, beyond which, a worn path leads up to the grassy summit plateau of Harter Fell. Once again, the views across to High Street are excellent, particularly so if you drop a short distance down Harter Fell's northern slopes. For first-time visitors to Harter Fell (778m/2552 feet), the sight of a cairn adorned with enough iron posts to attract scrap dealers comes as quite a surprise. In fact with a little imagination, accompanied by swirling mist, the cairn takes on the appearance of a fully-armed medieval Japanese warrior!

Survey column near the top of Tarn Crag.

Shipman Knotts.

Descending Shipman Knotts.

The summit cairn on Harter Fell.

The next section of the walk also forms part of the Kentmere Horseshoe and you are likely to see more walkers along this southern leg. Heading south from Harter Fell a fence, then a wall, points the way down The Knowe to a peaty hollow from where a broad, grassy ridge leads over Brown Howe to Kentmere Pike its high point at 730m/2395 feet. Although these fells are very grassy, Kentmere Pike's eastern flanks are much rockier with the impressive Raven Crag and Goat Scar overlooking the head of Longsleddale.

Continuing down open moorland, the craggy top of Shipman Knotts is reached from where you have a fine view back up the valley of the River Sprint and across the Kentmere valley to the shapely trio of Froswick, Ill Bell and Yoke. Eventually, steep broken slopes sweep down to a pass crossed by an ancient track connecting Kentmere with Longsleddale. The walk ends with a gentle stroll left down the bridleway past Sadgill Wood and over the packhorse bridge.

INFORMATION
Start/Finish: Sadgill, GR: 484056
Distance: 15km/9.3 miles.
Walking Time/total climb: 5 hours/910m (2985 feet).
Grading: Moderate; mainly rugged fell walking on good paths but also some boggy sections. Good navigation skills needed in misty conditions.
Maps: OS Explorer OL 5 & 7; Harvey Superwalker, Lakeland East.
Refreshments: Various pubs and cafés in Kendal.
Public Transport: No public transport to Sadgill.

The head of Coppermines valley.

Ascending Brown Pike from Blind Tarn backed by Coniston Old Man.

6   SOUTHERN FELLS

The compact Coniston range, with its impressive coves, tarns and rocky ridges, is the most southerly group of Lakeland fells. Coniston Old Man is the highest point, and for many walkers is usually the objective of the day, although all of the tops from Brown Pike to Wetherlam are linked by broad ridges, and can be visited in one long outing.

The fells overlook Coniston village and once you leave the streets of grey, stone houses you soon realise that slate quarrying and mining have played an important part in the area's past. Evidence of mineral mines are visible, particularly in the Coppermines Valley, which date back to Roman times, eventually closing at the end of the nineteenth century.

Just south of the village is the beautiful Coniston Water, on whose north-eastern shore stands Brantwood, once home to the celebrated Victorian artist, essayist and critic John Ruskin, who lived there from 1872 until his death in 1900. It was Ruskin who wrote: 'Mountains are the beginning and end of all natural scenery.' There is a Ruskin museum in Coniston, which covers much of his life, and also shows the history of the village.

Coniston's other famous son was Arthur Ransome, author of the children's classic *Swallows and Amazons*. He lived here from 1930 until he died in 1967. The surrounding area played an important fictional role in the book, with Peel Island on Coniston Water becoming 'Wild Cat Island'. The sheltered lake can be explored on the National Trust's steam yacht, *Gondola*, maybe stopping off to visit Brantwood on the way.

With its regular bus services, Coniston is an ideal centre for exploring the surrounding fells. There is plenty of accommodation including hotels, B&Bs, two youth hostels, one in the village, the other in Coppermines valley, and a lakeside campsite at Coniston Hall.

Above: *Wetherlam from Little Langdale Tarn.*

Far left: *Dow Crag from the Walna Scar Road.*

Left: *Low Water overlooked by Brim Fell.*

The Coniston fells across Coniston Water.

WALK 21 AROUND THE CONISTON CREST

The Old Man of Coniston must be the most tunnelled and quarried mountain in Lakeland, and has provided slate and copper for centuries. Despite the slopes being extensively ravaged by Man, the peak has great character. It stands proud over Coniston village from where this superb high-level ridge walk starts. The circuit links the summits of Brown Pike, Dow Crag, The Old Man, Brim Fell, Swirl How and Wetherlam, offering walkers a long outing across broad ridges and through dramatic scenery.

Coniston to The Old Man

Starting from the centre of Coniston, a narrow lane just left of Church Beck's bridge, leads past the Sun Inn and the old railway station car park. The lane climbs steeply up to an alternative parking area at the start of the Walna Scar road, an old packhorse route linking Coniston with Ravenglass. The popular route up the Old Man starts opposite the car park along an old miners' track heading between Stubthwaite Crag and The Bell, before turning sharp left for the summit up steep rocky slopes above Low Water.

Our way though lies along the Walna Scar road, which continues as a rough track beyond the car park. Just before the track crosses a bridge over a beck from Goat's Water, a well-used path, and an alternative way to the tops, branches right by a cairn and climbs the grassy slopes to Goat's Water overlooked by the frowning buttresses of Dow Crag. The Walna Scar track is followed further as it climbs across the southern flanks of Brown Pike. Here a footpath branches off right eventually climbing up to the top of Brown Pike (682m/2238 feet). A more direct approach is up its east ridge overlooking the lovely Blind Tarn.

140

The Scafell range from Dow Crag.

The summit of Dow Crag at dusk.

Ahead, a ridge climbs north over Buck Pike to the rocky top of Dow Crag (778m/2552 feet). Situated high above steep buttresses, this is a wonderful eyrie where you can really appreciate fine, panoramic views especially across Dunnerdale to the Scafell range and east to The Old Man. Dow Crag's cliffs consist of five impressive buttresses cleft by dark gullies and are named in alphabetical order from left to right. The cliffs are forever linked with the early beginnings of Lakeland rock climbing, where famous mountaineers such as W.P. Haskett-Smith, Cecil Slingsby, Owen Glynne Jones and the Abraham brothers have left their mark. It was Haskett-Smith who made the first climb on Dow Crag as early as 1886.

The north ridge of Dow Crag sweeps down and round to the dip at Goat's Hause then continues up and around the valley rim to the large summit cairn of Coniston

Dow Crag and Goat's Water.

Leaving Brim Fell.

Old Man standing on a plinth of rock at 803m/2634 feet. The sudden bird's-eye-view of Low Water in a hollow encircled by crags and steep slopes on the northern side of the Old Man is stunning. On sunny days the copper salts dissolved in the water impart a bright, peacock blue to the tarn. From the summit there are great views of high fells to the north, and on a clear day you can look south and east over the estuaries of Kent, Leven and Duddon and along the full length of Coniston Water.

The Old Man to Coniston

Leaving the top of the Old Man it's just a gentle amble north to the small cairn at the top of Brim Fell (796m/2612 feet). This spot can also be reached by one of the best long scrambling outings in the area; a 457m/1500 feet combination of an ascent of Low Water Beck, followed by a clamber up a broken ridge on the slabby buttress above Low Water, finishing just a stone's throw from the top of Brim Fell.

Continuing in the same direction, the path descends gently to the dip at Levers Hause from where you can peer right to Levers Water backed by Coniston village and lake. Beyond the dip the main path climbs north up to Swirl How's summit cairn at 802m/2631 feet. If time permits then an easy out-and-back detour round the rim of Calf Cove to Great Carrs and Grey Friar is highly recommended.

On the way to Great Carrs you pass close by a cairn, wooden cross and a few pieces of aircraft wreckage, including part of the landing gear. It marks the site where a Halifax bomber crashed in October 1944 while on a night flying exercise, killing all eight crew members. The rest of the wreckage is scattered down Broad Slack to the east.

Ahead the terrain changes dramatically and broad grassy slopes are now exchanged for a plunging rocky ridge known as the Prison Band. The path weaves its way down the crags to the dip at Swirl Hause, from where there is an easy escape route right down to Levers Water and the Coppermines valley. Beyond the dip the path rises steeply to bypass the minor top of Black Sails across its left shoulder overlooking the Greenburn valley.

Scrambling up Low Water Beck.

Storm clouds over Wetherlam.

Traversing up right, the path soon rejoins the broad ridge leading up to the large cairn at the rocky top of Wetherlam (762m/2500 feet). This is yet another magnificent vantage point for picking out all those familiar hill profiles arcing from the Helvellyn massif in the north-east, to Blencathra and Skiddaw, and round to the Scafell range.

A cairned path leads south-east from the summit down an easy shoulder overlooking large cliffs to the left; particularly impressive is Hen Crag, from where you have views down to Tilberthwaite. The slopes eventually level off at a small tarn on Red Gill Head before descending south along the ridge of Lad Stones. A green path eventually zigzags down to some cottages and the road through the Coppermines valley. Here you can see the scars of the valley's industrial past, firstly mined for copper, which was at its peak in the 1850s, and later quarrying for slate. At the height of mining activity, more than 600 men were employed in the valley.

Just down the road is Miners' Bridge from where a path on the right bank of Church Beck leads through woods, then across fields to arrive in Coniston beside the Sun Inn.

Scrambling up Brim Fell from Low Water.

INFORMATION

Start/Finish: Coniston village car park, GR: 304975 or the car park at the old railway station above the Sun Inn.

Distance: 19.5km/12 miles.

Walking Time/total climb: 6-8 hours/ 1300m (4265 feet).

Grading: Difficult; a high level fell walk on mainly good paths and some steep rocky ridges.

Maps: OS Explorer OL 6; Harvey Super-walker, Lakeland South West.

Refreshments: Sun Hotel and Black Bull Hotel and cafés in Coniston.

Public Transport: Railway station at Windermere with connecting bus service to Coniston.

Wetherlam from the top of Swirl How.

Swirl How and the Prison Band ridge from Wetherlam.

North from Wetherlam to Birk Fell.